Soccer Nutrition:

A Step-by-Step Guide on How to Fuel a Great Performance

Dylan Joseph

Soccer Nutrition:
A Step-by-Step Guide on How to Fuel a Great Performance
By: Dylan Joseph
© 2021
All Rights Reserved

WAIT!

Wouldn't it be nice to have an easy one-page summary of the key points covered in this book? Well, here is your chance!

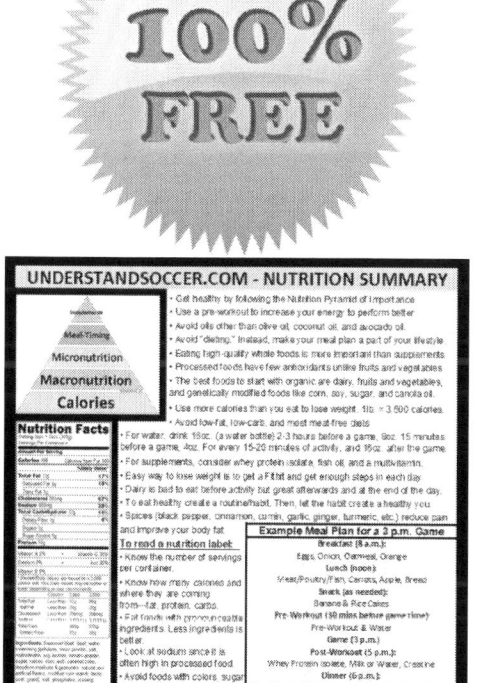

Go to this Link for an **Instant** One-Page Printout:
UnderstandSoccer.com/free-printout

This FREE checklist is simply a thank you for purchasing this book. This one-page summary will ensure that the tips in this book help you become the best soccer player you can be!

Soccer Nutrition:
A Step-by-Step Guide on How to Fuel a Great Performance
All Rights Reserved
March 18, 2021
Copyright © 2021 Understand, LLC
Dylan@UnderstandSoccer.com
Printed in the United States of America

No part of this book may be reproduced or transmitted in any form or by any means, electronic or mechanical, including but not limited to photocopying, recording, or by any information storage and retrieval system, without the written permission of Understand, LLC.

The information provided within this book is for general informational and educational purposes only and does not constitute an endorsement of any websites or other sources. If you apply the ideas contained in this book, then you are taking full responsibility for your actions. There are no representations or warranties, expressed or implied, about the completeness, accuracy, reliability, suitability, or availability of the information, products, or services contained in this book for any purpose. The author does not assume and hereby disclaims all liability to any party for any loss, damage, or disruption caused by errors or omissions, whether the errors or omissions are a result of accident, negligence, or any other cause.

Any use of this information is at your own risk. The methods described in this book are the author's personal thoughts. They are not intended to be a definitive set of instructions for everyone. You may discover that other methods and materials accomplish the same result. This book contains information that is intended to help readers become better-informed consumers of soccer knowledge. Always consult your physician for your individual needs before beginning any new exercise or nutrition program. This book is not intended to be a substitute for the medical advice of a licensed physician.

Table of Contents

Dedication ...... - 4 -
Preface ...... - 5 -
Introduction ...... - 12 -
Nutrition Pyramid of Importance ...... - 14 -
Making a Routine ...... - 28 -
Why "Dieting" is Bad ...... - 36 -
Pre-Game and In-Game Nutrition ...... - 39 -
Supplements ...... - 43 -
Post-Game Nutrition ...... - 48 -
Ronaldo's and Messi's Meal Plans ...... - 53 -
What to Eat on Non-Training/Playing Days ...... - 58 -
Sports Drinks vs. Water? ...... - 62 -
General Nutrition Tips ...... - 66 -
Weight Loss ...... - 71 -
How to Read a Nutrition Label ...... - 79 -
Organic, GMO, Vegan/Vegetarian, Gluten-Free, and Paleo Diets ...... - 86 -
Herbs and Spices ...... - 92 -
Which Oils Should You Use? ...... - 98 -
Afterword ...... - 105 -
Free Book! ...... - 107 -
About the Author ...... - 108 -
Thank You for Reading! ...... - 111 -
Glossary ...... - 112 -
Acknowledgments ...... - 117 -

Dedication

This book is dedicated to you, the soccer player, who cares enough about your success that you are willing to read a book to improve your nutrition to help yourself succeed in soccer. Learning is exceptionally noble and speaks volumes to the person you are.

Also, this book is dedicated to Joe Weider for all his work to improve the fitness and nutrition of athletes around the world.

Preface

Having great eating habits can be the difference from average performances and lifting the trophy at the end of the season. Because your body is fueled by what you eat, eating the correct foods at the right times will help you succeed on the soccer field. This book gives you the tips, tricks, tweaks, and techniques to learn what things make the biggest difference for a soccer player, it will help you understand how to make eating healthy a habit that you do not even have to think about, and how to get an edge over your competition.

INDIVIDUAL SOCCER PLAYER'S PYRAMID

(Pyramid diagram with MINDSET, NUTRITION, PARENTING, SLEEP labeled on the sides. From top to bottom: Tryouts, Fitness, Defending | Shooting & Finishing | Dribbling & Foot Skills, Passing & Receiving. Below the pyramid: COACHING, DRILLS, POSITIONS)

If you are looking to improve your skills, your child's confidence, or your players' abilities, then it is essential to understand where this book fits into the bigger picture of developing a soccer player. In the image, the most critical field-specific skills to work on are at the base of the Individual Soccer Player's Pyramid. This pyramid is a quality outline to improve an individual soccer player's game. All the elements in the pyramid, and the items surrounding it, play a meaningful part in becoming a better player, but certain skills should be read and mastered first before moving on to the others.

You will notice that passing and receiving is at the foundation of the pyramid. This is because if you can receive and make a pass in soccer, then you will be a useful teammate. Even though you may not consistently score, dispossess the other team, or dribble through several opponents, you will still have the fundamental tools needed to play the sport and contribute to your team.

As you move one layer up, you find yourself with a decision to make on how to progress. Specifically, the pyramid is created with you in mind because each soccer player and each soccer position have different needs. Therefore, your choice regarding which path to take first is dictated by the position you play and more importantly, by the position that you want to play. In soccer and life, just because you are in a particular spot, position, or even a job, it does not mean that you must stay there forever if that is not your choice. However, it is not recommended to refuse playing a position if you are not in the exact role you want. It takes time to develop the skills that will allow you to make a shift from one position to another.

If you want to become a forward, then consider starting your route on the second layer of the pyramid with shooting and finishing. As your abilities to shoot increase, your coach will notice your new finishing skills and will be more likely to move you up the field (if you are not a forward already). Be sure to communicate to the coach that you desire to be moved up the field to a more offensive position, which will increase your chances, as well. If you are already a forward, then dive deep into this topic to ensure you become the leading scorer; first on your team, and then in the entire league. Notice that shooting and finishing is considered to be less critical than passing and receiving. This is because you must pass the ball up the field before you can take a shot on net.

Otherwise, you can start by progressing to dribbling and foot skills from passing and receiving because the proper technique is crucial to dribble the ball well. It is often necessary for a soccer player to use a skill to protect the ball from the other team or to advance the ball up the field to place their team in a favorable situation to score. The selection of this route is often taken first by midfielders and occasionally by forwards.

Defending is another option to proceed from passing and receiving. Keeping the other team off the scoreboard is not an easy task. Developing a defender's mindset, learning which way to push a forward, understanding how to position your body, knowing when to foul, and using the correct form for headers is critical to a defender on the back line who wants to prevent goals.

Finish all three areas in the second layer of the pyramid before progressing up the pyramid. Dribbling and defending the ball (not just shooting) are useful for an attacker; shooting and defending (not just dribbling) are helpful for a midfielder, while shooting and dribbling (not just defending) are helpful for a defender. Having a well-rounded knowledge of the skills needed for the different positions is important for all soccer players. It is especially essential for those soccer players who are looking to change positions in the future. Shooting and finishing, dribbling and foot skills, as well as defending are often more beneficial for soccer players to learn first, so focus on these before spending time on the upper areas of the pyramid. In addition, reading about each of these areas will help you understand what your opponent wants to do.

Once you have improved your skills in the first and second tiers of the pyramid, you can move up to fitness. It is difficult to go through a passing/dribbling/finishing drill for a few minutes without being out of breath. However, as you practice everything below the fitness category in the pyramid, your fitness and strength will naturally increase. Performing technical drills allows soccer players to increase their fitness naturally. This reduces the need to focus exclusively on running for fitness.

Coming from the perspective of both a soccer player and trainer, I know that constantly focusing on running is not as fulfilling and does not create long-lasting improvements, whereas emphasizing shooting capabilities, foot skills, and defending knowledge creates long-lasting change. Often, coaches who focus on running their players in practice are also coaches who want to improve their team but have limited knowledge of many of the soccer-specific topics that would quickly increase their players' abilities. Not only does fitness in soccer include your endurance; it also addresses your ability to run with agility and speed and to develop strength and power, while using stretching to improve your flexibility. All these tools put together leads to a well-rounded soccer player.

Similar to the tier below it, you should focus on the fitness areas that will help you specifically, while keeping all the topics in mind. For example, you may be a smaller soccer player who wants to put on some muscle mass. In this case, you should emphasize weight training so that you can gain the muscle needed to avoid being pushed off the ball. However, you should still stretch before and after a lifting workout or soccer practice/game to ensure that you are limber and flexible enough to recover quickly and avoid injuries.

Maybe you are a soccer player in your 20s, 30s, or 40s. Then, emphasizing your flexibility would do a world of good to ensure you keep playing soccer for many more years. However, doing a few sets of push-ups, pull-ups, squats, lunges, sit-ups, etc. per week will help you maintain or gain a desirable physique.

Furthermore, you could be in the prime of your career in high school, college, or at the pro level, which means that obtaining the speed and endurance needed to run for 90+ minutes is the most essential key to continue pursuing your soccer aspirations.

Finally, we travel to the top of the pyramid, which involves tryouts. Although tryouts occur only 1-2 times per year, they have a huge impact on whether you will make the team or get left out of the lineup. Tryouts can cause intense anxiety if you do not know the keys to make sure that you stand out from your competitors and are very confident from the start.

If you have not read the *Understand Soccer* series book, *Soccer Training*, then it is highly recommended that you do so to gain the general knowledge of crucial topics within all the areas of the pyramid. Picking up a copy of the book will act as a good gauge to see how much you know about each topic, which will then help determine if a book that was later in the series written about a specific subject in the soccer pyramid will be beneficial for you.

The last portion of the pyramid are the areas that surround it. Although these are not skills and topics that can be addressed by your physical abilities, they each play key roles in rounding out a complete soccer player. For example, having one or more supportive parent(s)/guardian(s) is beneficial, as they can transport the child to games, and provide the needed equipment and the fees for the team and individual training, as well as encouragement. It is also very helpful to have a quality coach whose teachings and drills will help the individual learn how their performance and skills fit into the team's big picture.

Sleeping enough is critical to having enough energy during practices and on game days, in addition to recovering from training and games. Appropriate soccer nutrition will increase a soccer player's energy and endurance, help them achieve the ideal physique, and significantly aid in their recovery.

Understanding soccer positions will help you determine if a specific role is well-suited for your skills. It is important to know there are additional types of specific positions, not just forwards, midfielders, and defenders. A former or current professional player in the same position as you can provide guidance on the requirements to effectively play that position.

Finally, you must develop a mindset that will leave you unshakable. This mindset will help you prepare for game situations, learn how to deal with other players, and be mentally tough enough to not worry about circumstances that you cannot control, such as the type of field you play on, the officiating, or the weather.

The pyramid is a great visual aid to consider when choosing what areas to focus on next as a soccer player, coach, or parent. However, remember that a team's pyramid may look slightly different based on which tactics the players can handle and which approach the coach decides to use for games. Now that you know where this book plays into the bigger picture, let us begin.

Remember that if there are any words or terms whose meaning you are unsure of; you can feel free to reference the glossary at the back of the book.

Finally, if you enjoy this book, please leave a review on Amazon to let me know.

Introduction

The purpose of this book is to provide you with the nutritional knowledge needed to perform better on gameday, recover quickly after training, and gain muscle and lose fat to boost your confidence. This book reveals the key areas of nutrition, which will provide you the greatest results in the shortest time, and it will help you learn how to turn them into habits without using much energy. Keep in mind that this book is geared towards the demands of a soccer player, as their nutritional needs differ from those of the general population.

As you read this book, please understand that I am not a certified dietitian. However, I am a person with tens of thousands of hours of experience on the field, in the weight room, and in the kitchen. Currently, I have read well over 250 nutrition, fitness, bodybuilding, and health magazines, in addition to over 40 nutrition, food science, and weight training books. Having placed the insights into practice, I have realized there is much more to be learned in "doing" than only in the reading/listening about a subject.

This book provides an understanding of nutrition for a soccer player but applying the concepts is what offers the real knowledge. You can understand a lot from reading. However, applying what you read is how you will take yourself from a novice level to an amateur level, from an amateur level to a proficient level, and finally from a proficient level to a professional level.

Personally, I started out as a chubby child who liked junk food, then became too skinny because I did not eat enough food, and now I have finally found the sweet spot. I have maintained an athletic body type for over 15 years after I committed to eating right and consistently exercising. I reveal this not to impress you but to express that having a good nutrition plan is critical for being healthy, looking the way you want to look, and increasing your performance on the field and your confidence off the field.

If at any point you feel the information is in this book is too detailed, do not worry. Two of my four editors did as well and recommended that I take out a considerable amount of the nutrition science. Given that some of you reading this will also want the science behind the advice, I have included the detailed information in a way that is reader-friendly. However, for those of you who begin to read this book and feel there is too much information, I would suggest focusing on the images and any sentences that are bolded. Viewing the pictures/charts/graphs and understanding the bolded summary sentence of each paragraph will make the information easier to consume.

With that in mind, countless hours of experimenting, trials, and errors have occurred to develop what works best for a soccer player. Neither eating right nor exercising alone is enough to have both a great-looking body and healthy organs. However, combining each will allow them to work better.

Chapter 1

Nutrition Pyramid of Importance

Let us face it, you have only so many hours a day, most of which are spent unrelated to food. As with all things, the more time you spend on something, the more knowledge you will gain, and the better you will become. However, just like how practicing passing and receiving is more important for a soccer player than practicing bicycle/overhead kicks, there are certain aspects of nutrition which will provide bigger results in a shorter period of time. Therefore, make your time count by ensuring that you understand the Nutrition Pyramid of Importance.

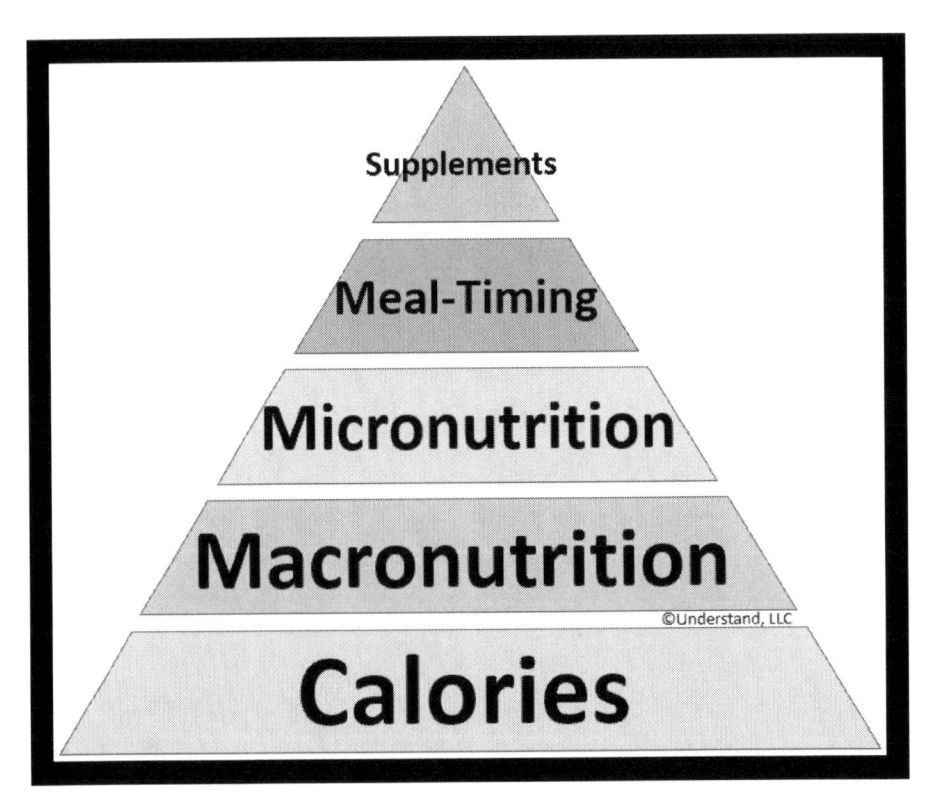

To receive the most from your soccer nutrition, it is so important that you spend time on the more critical areas—like consuming enough calories—and are not so worried about things which bring significantly less value for your time and money. A close friend of mine, Michael Mroczka, would argue with me for years about the number of calories I consume being more important than the quality of those calories when striving to reach a goal. Sadly, sometimes, I can be stubborn and because I had read hundreds of nutrition books, fitness magazines, health encyclopedias, and articles on eating healthy, I believed that eating healthier foods would provide more benefit than watching the number of calories I ate.

Then, three months before my wedding, I hired a dietician to advise me on my eating leading up to my marriage, so I would be in the best shape of my life when I went to Jamaica for our honeymoon. Now, keep in mind that I had been eating extremely healthy and exercising a ton over the 10 years prior—not to mention I had done many at-home DVD workout programs, like P90X, Insanity, Body Beast, etc. Sure enough, the dietician's main aim for my entire 12-week meal plan was focused around making sure I took in the right number of calories for my desired physique and met the guidelines for the macronutrients of carbohydrates, fat, and protein. When hiring the dietician who knew my extensive background in nutrition, I told him to tell me what I needed to do, and not what I wanted to hear him say. So, he stayed consistent about how important the calories and macronutrition were.

I had paid him a lot to guide me, so I was committed to following his advice, no matter how much I thought the quality of the food, taking supplements, and meal timing was more important. Sure enough, at the end of the 12-week period, I looked the best and most defined I have ever looked in my life. From that point on, I realized I was wrong and that the Nutrition Pyramid of Importance was key in determining how I spent my time.

For soccer players, understanding the Nutrition Pyramid of Importance will give you an advantage over players who do not care about nutrition, and players who care about nutrition but focus too much on taking tons of supplements and eating eight times a day.

Let us now discuss each area of the Nutrition Pyramid of Importance and how they will make a significant impact. This is the longest chapter in the book because it will explain the various parts of food to ensure that you can easily follow along with the rest of the chapters.

Calories

When building a pyramid (or your body), having a solid foundation will make it easier to build all other layers. At the base of the Nutrition Pyramid of Importance are calories. A calorie is how we measure the amount of energy there is in food. **Like how producing our world's energy from coal impacts the environment differently than energy from wind, sun, or water, the energy from carbohydrates differs from protein or fat, and a calorie from a candy bar is different when compared to a calorie from organic brown rice.** Here are the recommended guidelines for the number of calories to consume each day:

MALES

AGE	Sedentary	Moderately Active	Active
2	1,000	1,000	1,000
3	1,000	1,400	1,400
4	1,200	1,400	1,600
5	1,200	1,400	1,600
6	1,400	1,600	1,800
7	1,400	1,600	1,800
8	1,400	1,600	2,000
9	1,600	1,800	2,000
10	1,600	1,800	2,200
11	1,800	2,000	2,200
12	1,800	2,200	2,400
13	2,000	2,200	2,600
14	2,000	2,400	2,800
15	2,200	2,600	3,000
16-18	2,400	2,800	3,200
19-20	2,600	2,800	3,000
21-25	2,400	2,800	3,000
26-30	2,400	2,600	3,000
31-35	2,400	2,600	3,000
36-40	2,400	2,600	2,800
41-45	2,200	2,600	2,800
46-50	2,200	2,400	2,800
51-55	2,200	2,400	2,800
56-60	2,200	2,400	2,600
61-65	2,000	2,400	2,600
66-70	2,000	2,200	2,600
71-75	2,000	2,200	2,600
76 and up	2,000	2,200	2,400

Source: Health.gov

FEMALES

AGE	Sedentary	Moderately Active	Active
2	1,000	1,000	1,000
3	1,000	1,200	1,400
4	1,200	1,400	1,400
5	1,200	1,400	1,600
6	1,200	1,400	1,600
7	1,200	1,600	1,800
8	1,400	1,600	1,800
9	1,400	1,600	1,800
10	1,400	1,800	2,000
11	1,600	1,800	2,000
12	1,600	2,000	2,200
13	1,600	2,000	2,200
14	1,800	2,000	2,400
15	1,800	2,000	2,400
16-18	1,800	2,000	2,400
19-20	2,000	2,200	2,400
21-25	2,000	2,200	2,400
26-30	1,800	2,000	2,400
31-35	1,800	2,000	2,200
36-40	1,800	2,000	2,200
41-45	1,800	2,000	2,200
46-50	1,800	2,000	2,200
51-55	1,600	1,800	2,200
56-60	1,600	1,800	2,200
61-65	1,600	1,800	2,000
66-70	1,600	1,800	2,000
71-75	1,600	1,800	2,000
76 and up	1,600	1,800	2,000

Source: Health.gov

If you want to be even more precise, check out: https://www.calculator.net/calorie-calculator.html or simply Google "calorie calculator." Here, you can put in your exact height and weight too, to give you an even closer idea of the estimated guideline for how many calories you should consume each day to maintain your weight. Remember that it can vary from day-to-day, too. **For example, you should eat more on a day where you have a soccer tournament consisting of three games. You should eat less on a day in the offseason when you do not play soccer or exercise.**

Now, you may be thinking that counting your calories can take a lot of time. Yes, it can. I sometimes spent two hours a day preparing/measuring food during my 12-week meal plan prior to getting married. This is too time consuming for most soccer players but understanding how to read a nutrition label (covered in a later chapter), and how to estimate the number of calories and protein that you have eaten in a day will reveal whether your eating habits will help you perform better or hold you back from success.

Macronutrients

Macronutrients are the carbs, fats, proteins, fibers, and fluids needed to function. Macronutrients are needed in large quantities from food. Which ones you consume and when you consume them can be the difference from having a six-pack and lean physique or an average physique which goes unnoticed.

Carbs (carbohydrates) are broken down by the body to provide energy from sugars, starches, and cellulose. For carbs, it is good to classify them into two categories: fast-digesting and slow-digesting. Fast-digesting carbs are the things like white bread, white rice, and white pasta which your body can quickly turn into blood sugar (glycogen), which causes a sharp spike in your body's blood sugar. This can be good when you are about to perform in a soccer game or while drinking a post-game protein shake. However, it can be terrible for your body at other parts of the day when you do not need elevated energy/sugar levels and do not want to experience a "crash" of energy. Foods like oatmeal, whole wheat pasta, sweet potatoes, brown rice, and whole grain bread are much slower digesting and lead to sustained levels of energy without having spikes and dips in energy.

Fats (lipids) are especially important to provide your body energy, support cell growth, protect your organs, keep your body warm, absorb fat-soluble nutrients, and produce important hormones. Fats come in four main types: 1) Monounsaturated 2) Polyunsaturated 3) Saturated 4) Trans. Both monounsaturated and polyunsaturated fats are healthful. Fats from nuts, seeds, olives, algae, and fatty fish will provide the unsaturated fat needed. These types of fats are liquid at room temperature.

Saturated fats are solid at room temperature and can be found in palm and coconut oils, cheese, butter, and red meat. Currently, the health community is torn on whether these are healthy fats or not. Personally, it is hard to say that a coconut is unhealthy for you. There are so many benefits of coconut oil that I could write an entire book on them. Feel free to do additional research on the subject, but I honestly believe based on numerous studies that high-quality organic cheeses, butter, and red meats in moderation will lead to a healthier lifestyle for a soccer player than avoiding them entirely.

Also, there are trans-fats. There are some naturally occurring trans-unsaturated fatty acids in meat and milk fat. **However, the true "villain" of fat is trans-fat, which is chemically created in a factory by hydrogenating oils.** This means that food companies turn liquid oils into solids to increase the shelf life and flavor of the foods which contain them. There is currently a large trend in the fitness industry to avoid these fats because they are linked to heart disease. The trick to seeing if there is trans-fat in a packaged good is to look at the ingredients list for any partially or fully hydrogenated oils and stay as far away from them as you can.

Like carbohydrates, protein can be viewed by how quickly it digests. **First, protein is made up of many amino acids, which help aid in normal cell function, muscle growth, enzyme creation, hormone production, and they can be used for energy.** Whey protein—which comes from milk—is one of the fastest-digesting proteins. It can be purchased separately from milk, too. Casein protein—which also comes from milk—is one of the slowest-digesting proteins. The protein from fish/shellfish is faster digesting than the protein from beef, while chicken/turkey falls in between. Think of protein as your muscle's building blocks.

Lastly, the final macronutrient we will cover is fiber. Technically, fiber is a carbohydrate. However, it is a carb which the body cannot digest. **Fiber is important for regulating digestion, regular bowel movements, helps keep you feeling fuller for** longer, **improves your cholesterol levels, regulates blood sugar levels, and prevents diseases like diabetes and heart disease.** Fiber is often classified in one of two ways: 1) Soluble 2) Insoluble. Soluble fiber dissolves in water and in gastrointestinal fluids when it enters your body's stomach and intestines. It changes into a gel-like substance that bacteria in your body digests, releasing gases and a few calories. Insoluble fiber does not dissolve in water or in your body and remains unchanged as it moves through you before being pooped out. Because it is not digested at all, insoluble fiber is not a source of calories your body can use for energy. Think of insoluble fiber as a cleaner which travels through your body scrubbing down the walls and leaving everything a little bit healthier. Soluble fiber is in oat bran, barley, nuts, seeds, beans, lentils, peas, and some fruits and vegetables. Insoluble fiber is in wheat bran, vegetables, whole grains, etc.

If the explanations of each of these macronutrients seemed intense, do not worry. There is an even simpler way to remember what is good to eat and what is not: **If it was made in a factory, then it is probably not good for you**. In general, fruits, vegetables, organic grains, sustainably raised meats, nuts, seeds, beans, and fish are good for you. They can be found in nature. Processed foods, packaged goods, and beverages are made by humans in a factory and usually are not good for you.

Micronutrients

A micronutrient is an element or substance that is required in trace amounts for normal growth and development. **Micronutrients can be broken down into the following key areas: vitamins, minerals, antioxidants, and phytonutrients.** Vitamins and minerals are necessary for good health. Antioxidants, anti-inflammatories, and phytonutrients are not vital, but they are beneficial for recovery, disease prevention, and pain reduction.

Consuming enough vitamins from food and supplements is essential because the body cannot produce enough on its own. **There are 13 essential vitamins, and they are all water-soluble or fat-soluble.** Fat-soluble vitamins can dissolve in fats and oils. They are absorbed along with fats in the diet and can be stored in the body's fat stores, which makes them the easier of the two for the body to store. Vitamins A, D, E, and K are fat-soluble. Water-soluble vitamins are carried throughout the body but are not stored in the body, so they must be taken in daily. Vitamins B and C are water-soluble.

Minerals are important for your body to stay healthy. Your body uses minerals to build your bones, to engage your muscles, create enzymes, produce hormones, regulate your blood, improve metabolism, and maintain your nervous system. **There are two kinds of minerals: 1) Macrominerals 2) Trace Minerals.** They include calcium, phosphorus, magnesium, sodium, potassium, chloride, and sulfur. You only need small amounts of trace minerals. They include iron, manganese, copper, iodine, zinc, cobalt, fluoride, and selenium. Your body needs larger quantities of macrominerals than trace minerals.

Antioxidants are literally "anti" oxidants. Oxidants are produced inside your body and outside in the environment, and they can react with other elements in your body, such as protein, DNA, and fats. The oxidants will damage your body and cause diseases like cancer, and inflammation like arthritis. Therefore, antioxidants prevent damage from the oxidants. **Antioxidants slow or prevent damage to cells caused by free radicals, which are unstable molecules in your body.**

As an example, if grill marks are burned into your chicken breast because you cooked it on the grill, the burned marks are oxidants in your body. However, if you eat some broccoli and blueberries with the chicken breast, then the antioxidants from the broccoli and blueberries would help fight the oxidants from the burned parts of the grilled chicken.

Antioxidants are mostly found in fruits and vegetables. However, in much smaller amounts, they can be found in nuts, whole grains, and some meats.

Phytonutrients are what give fruits and vegetables their color. Below, the different types of phytonutrients are listed. However, remembering their names is not important. **The key to remembering phytonutrients is knowing the five colors and making sure you are eating each of the colors**:

Red: Protects your DNA while preventing cancer and heart disease.
Foods: Apples, pomegranates, grapefruits, cherries, tomatoes, radishes, watermelons, raspberries, strawberries, etc.

Blue/Purple: Good for heart, brain, bones, and arteries. Fights cancer and promotes healthy aging.
Foods: Plums, red cabbage, beets, eggplants, red grapes, blueberries, blackberries, etc.

Green: Support eye health, arteries, lungs, and liver function. Helps to heal wounds and gum health.
Foods: Broccoli, kale, spinach, collard greens, kiwis, avocados, honeydews, lettuce, celery, etc.

White: Supports bone health, circulatory system, and arteries. Helps fight heart disease and cancer.
Foods: Onions, mushrooms, pears, garlic, cauliflower, parsnips, etc.

Yellow/Orange: Good for eye health, immune function, and healthy development.
Foods: Pineapples, peaches, papayas, bananas, lemons, carrots, pumpkins, sweet potatoes, nectarines, etc.

According to WebMD.com, four out of five people do not eat enough fruits and vegetables. **Although vegetables offer few proteins, fats, or carbs (other than fiber), they are vital for their fiber, vitamins, minerals, antioxidants, and phytonutrients.**

Meal Timing/Frequency

Meal timing is planning meals and snacks for specific times throughout the day (e.g., after a workout) to manage hunger, aid recovery, fuel performance, improve sleep, and build muscle.

Meal frequency is how often you eat. For example, the average person eats three times per day with one snack. However, a soccer player may find it better for their needs to eat five times per day and have a post-workout shake after training.

When meal timing, the most important thing to consider is whether you are consuming a post-workout shake if you are

training intensely, and to make sure that you are eating at least three meals per day that contain the number of calories you need to achieve your ideal physique.

Personally, I spent years training hard, eating six full meals per day, and drinking a post-workout shake after every training session. In hindsight, I realize that focusing on some of the soccer-specific skills like the "Big 3" foot skills and an emphasis on passing/receiving would have helped me more in becoming a better soccer player. *(**Note:** If you are interested in the "Big 3" foot skills, which will make the biggest impact on your soccer career, then grab a copy of the Understand Soccer series book, Soccer Dribbling & Foot Skills, to boost your confidence by becoming one of the best dribblers on your team!)*

Supplements

The last area of the Nutrition Pyramid of Importance belongs to supplements. First, a dietary supplement is a product taken by mouth which contains dietary ingredients, like vitamins, minerals, amino acids, herbs, and other substances. As a soccer player, you should be more concerned with soccer than nutrition, so it is important to focus on the few things which will give you the biggest results for the least amount of money and time spent. **Make sure that you are consuming a post-workout shake if you have intense training and want to either maintain your physique or improve it. Also, consume a fish-oil supplement, and a multivitamin.**

With multivitamins, think of them as an "insurance policy." Even if you are eating well, there is a chance you are missing a vitamin or trace mineral in your meal plan which you can easily obtain with an inexpensive multivitamin. Fish oil increases your good cholesterol, lowers your blood fat levels, decreases blood pressure, prevents plaque in the arteries, lubricates joints, and helps with brain development. Can you consume more than these? Absolutely! For years, I did too. However, a post-workout shake, fish oil, and multivitamin is the staple of a successful supplement plan for a soccer player.

To obtain the high-performing body that you want, the order of importance is:

1. Calories
2. Macronutrients
3. Micronutrients
4. Meal Frequency/Timing
5. Supplements

In summary, remember the 80/20 rule for nutrition, which states that 80% of your results come from 20% of the things you do. (**Note:** *If you want to achieve better results in less time, then you will enjoy the Understand Soccer series book, Soccer Mindset, which explains this principle in detail.*) Refer to this chapter or the glossary if you need a refresher on terms used throughout this book.

Chapter 2

Making a Routine

"We are what we repeatedly do. Excellence, therefore, is not an act, but a habit."
—Aristotle

Routines/habits are so important for finding success easily and achieving your goals. When you start something new, there is often excitement, nervousness, and worry. You are stressed about learning something new and must use a lot of mental energy to begin and maintain the process to learn about that new subject. Excitingly, this "10-foot hurdle" that most people place in their minds usually only seems like a 6-inch speed bump after you have gone over it. **Starting, committing, and learning the things you do not know is often the most difficult part of beginning, but once you have the hard stuff out of the way, it becomes much easier from there.**

However, the problem most people face is that they spend so much time and energy the first few occasions doing something which they think every single time will be like that and require a lot of effort. The following image shows how most people view things they know they should be doing, like eating healthy and exercising.

Effort You Think You Need

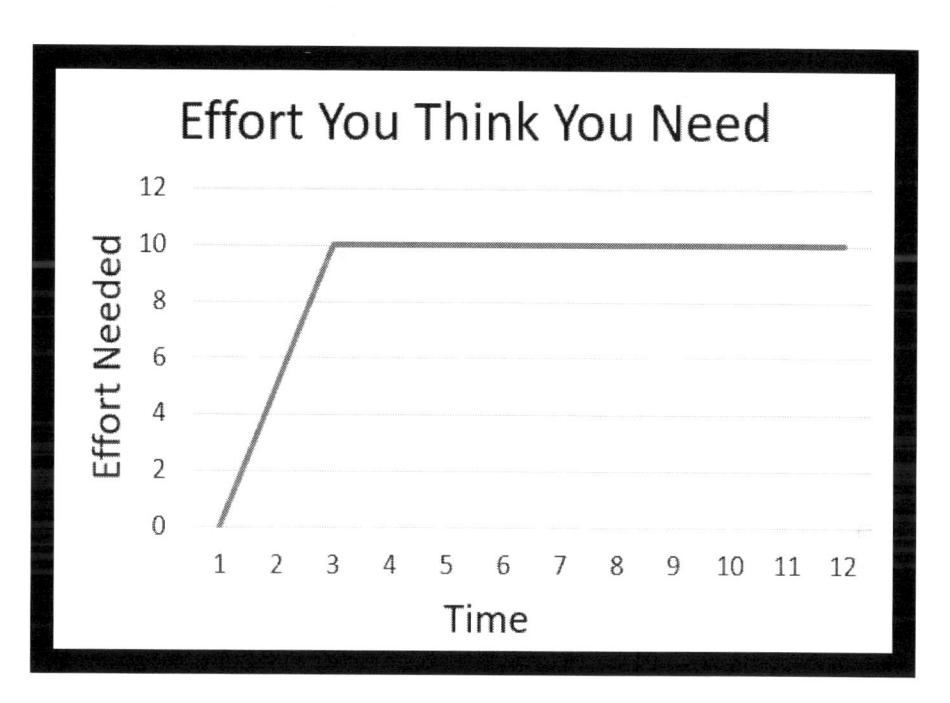

(Graph: Effort Needed vs. Time, showing effort rising sharply from 0 to 10 between time 1 and 3, then remaining constant at 10 through time 12.)

They give up without realizing they are close to getting to the point where it will be easy to maintain. Therefore, making a routine takes a considerable amount of effort to eat healthy, workout, read, obtain enough sleep, etc. **However, it becomes so easy to maintain once you have created a system (i.e., routine/process/habit).** Instead, look at the following image for what it really takes to keep a routine going.

Effort Needed

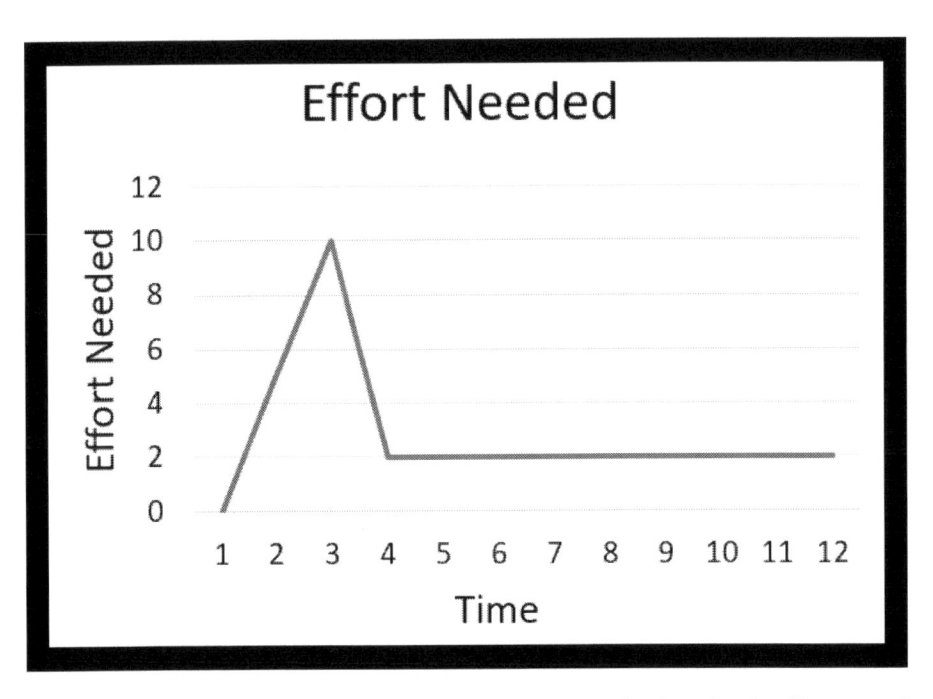

Notice in the image it takes a lot of physical effort and mental energy up front to learn everything and create the habit, but it only takes a bit of maintenance to keep the habit going. So, how long does it take to make a routine stick? Phillippa Lally, a health psychology researcher at University College London, published a study in the European Journal of Social Psychology on how long it takes to form a habit. The study examined the habits of participants over a 12-week period. Each person selected one new habit for the 12 weeks and reported every day on whether they did the behavior and how automatic the habit was.

Because the participants could choose their own habits, some were harder than others. At the end of the 12 weeks, the researchers analyzed the data to determine how long it took each person to go from starting a new behavior to automatically doing it. **On average, it 66 days for the new habit to stick.** It took less time for simpler tasks and longer for more difficult routines. Also, how long it took varied depending on the person and the circumstances. Therefore, 66 days or just over two months is a good target to set up the routine of preparing food and eating healthy. The researchers also found that it did not matter if the participants messed up now and then. Building better habits is not an all-or-nothing process when establishing the routine.

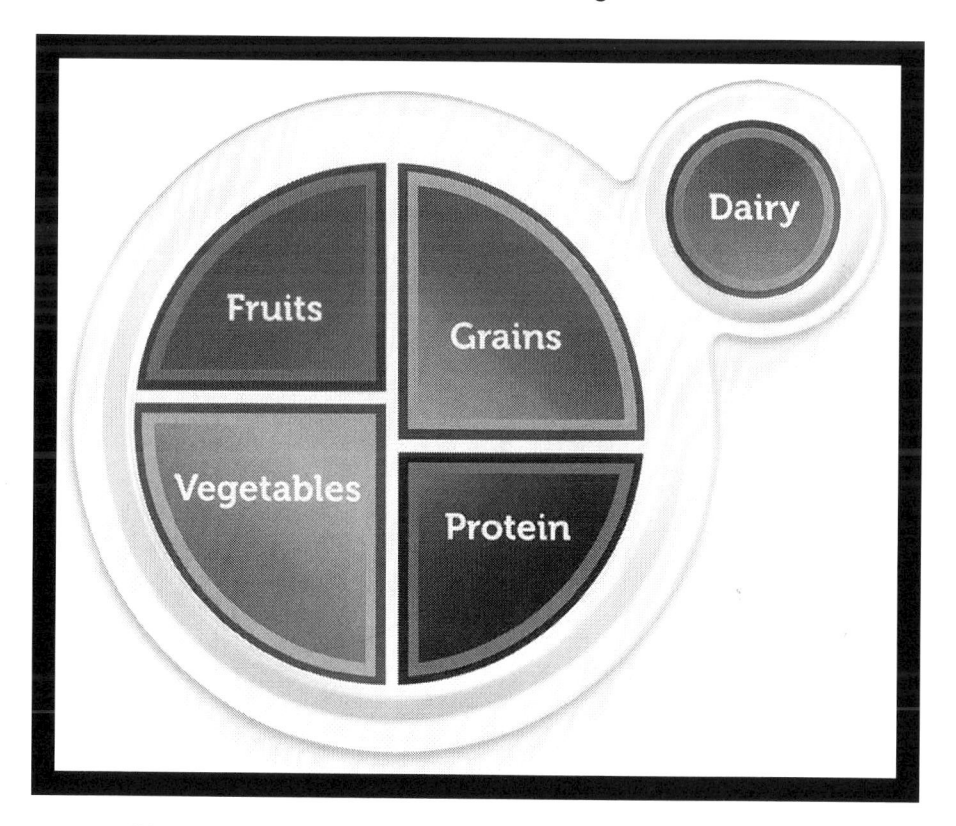

Given this book is about nutrition for the soccer player, let us talk about the most important routine in nutrition—what to eat and how much of it. The above image of "MyPlate" shows the breakout of how the U.S. Department of Agriculture recommends we portion our meals. **Remember that as a soccer player, your nutritional needs are different compared to the general population given that you exercise a lot more.** More exercise means you need more fuel to perform well and need to know when to eat each type of food to help with recovery without reducing your energy.

Therefore, look at the next image for a better recommendation for a soccer player. Feel free to change it based on your beliefs and what works best for your body.

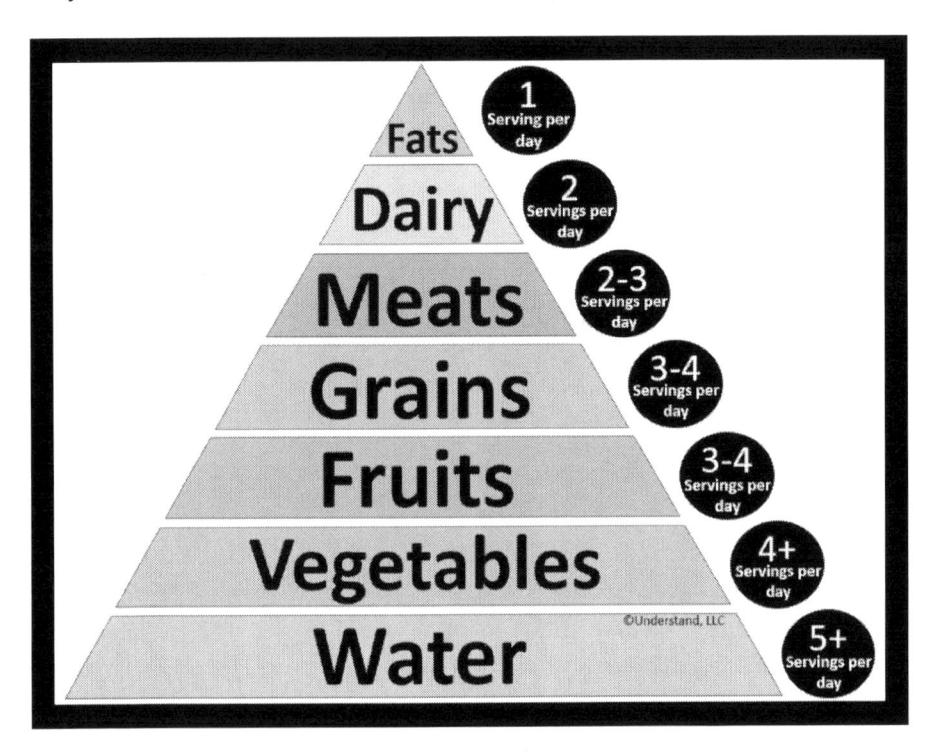

Food Group	Servings per day
Fats	1
Dairy	2
Meats	2-3
Grains	3-4
Fruits	3-4
Vegetables	4+
Water	5+

©Understand, LLC

Now, keep in mind that the serving size for an eight-year-old girl will be different than a 15-year-old boy, but fruits and vegetables should be a staple of every meal plan. Notice that the image is a pyramid, instead of a plate. A plate shows that you need to eat the same five food groups in every meal, **whereas the pyramid is not as restrictive and allows you to better plan meals around a training session or game with a serving size equal to one cup.** Also, the pyramid provides a few more things you should consume, including water as the foundation to ensure that your body will remain hydrated. You can be the healthiest eater on your team, but if you are dehydrated before the start of a game, then good luck outperforming someone who may have eaten worse foods but is well-hydrated!

Here are examples of things to eat from each "food group":

Healthy Fats – Coconut Oil, Extra-Virgin Olive Oil, & Avocado Oil
Dairy – Organic Milk, Greek Yogurt, & Minimally-Processed Cheese
Meats/Proteins – Beef, Poultry, Fish, Eggs, Beans, Nuts, & Seeds
Grains – Whole Grain Breads, Rice, Potatoes, Pasta, Organic Corn, & Steel-Cut Oatmeal
Fruits – Melons, Berries, Apples, Pears, Bananas, Peaches, Grapes, & Oranges
Vegetables – Lettuce, Carrots, Onions, Celery, Kale, Cabbage, Broccoli, Cauliflower, & Celery
Water – Not sports drinks, not flavored water beverages, and not soda pop.

Because this chapter is all about creating routines, let us discuss several ways to make it easier to eat healthy:

1. Cook in bulk (meal prep). By cooking in bulk, you will make it easier to bring food with you and always have something healthy prepared. Having so many other responsibilities (e.g., school, work, chores, family, friends, etc.) means that having food already made will make the routine of eating healthy even easier.

2. Keep easy-to-grab fruits and vegetables on hand. Having fruits and vegetables that take minimal or no time to prepare will make eating healthy more enjoyable. Having to prepare something versus grabbing a bag of chips makes it more likely that you grab the chips. However, picking between a bag of chips and an apple will increase your chances of making a more nutritious choice because you do not need prepare an apple, orange, box of raisins, carrots, or celery. For example, when I am in a rush, I can easily grab a banana, a few pieces of cabbage, a slice of organic whole-grain bread, and a handful of nuts. These easy-to-grab items do not need to be prepared; I just have to pick them up and take them with me.

3. Remove unhealthy food from the house. Getting unhealthy food out of your house will make it even easier to eat healthy because you will not need to use any willpower to choose between healthy and unhealthy foods if unhealthy foods are not an option, a concept known as "choice architecture." If you are the person who shops for your family, then make sure you do not go to the grocery store hungry. If you are not the person who shops for your family, then it will be a bit more difficult to get the food that you need. The best thing to do here is to communicate to the person who does the grocery shopping to please buy the healthier and easy-to-grab options you want. However, you may have a parent who does not want to buy healthier foods. Sadly, I had this, and it limited my food choices for a while in the house before my mom began buying foods that I would eat. You owe it to yourself, your health, and your performance on the soccer field to have the conversation with the person who buys the food.

4. Establish a routine for what your "normal" meal should look like. Knowing what a "normal" meal looks like makes it easier to know what should be on your plate. **A great meal involves one vegetable, one meat/protein, one fruit, and one grain (i.e., carb)**. Remember this! Honestly, 95% of my meals follow this easy-to-remember pattern, which takes away the hard work of choosing what to eat. If you know that your meals should have four key food groups, then it is easier to prepare/grab them. This habit will help you become a lot healthier and perform better on the soccer field. For example, as I am writing this chapter, I grabbed a stalk of celery (i.e., vegetable), walnuts (i.e., protein), raisins (i.e., fruit), and a sweet potato (i.e., grain/carb) to fuel the two hours of futsal (i.e., 5v5 indoor soccer) which I play on Fridays.

In summary, understanding how long it takes to form a routine, which habits will lead to a healthy lifestyle, and which rules will benefit you can make eating healthier quite easy to do. Remember that most habits take a considerable amount of energy and effort to establish but once created, they are usually easily maintained. Therefore, always do something with the intention of making it a habit. Creating habits like eating healthy, exercising regularly, getting enough sleep, and reading/listening to good books will eventually turn you into the person you want to be.

Chapter 3

Why "Dieting" is Bad

Your relationship with food and how you view it makes a big difference on how you feel and how you look. So many people have "Yo-Yo" diets where they will start a diet for a few weeks, eat a few junk-filled meals, say they need to be better, and then continue eating more meals void of nutrition to cover their poor feelings about falling off their diet. This continues for a few months and then they get back on another diet and change again. Honestly, just trying to explain that is exhausting and the Yo-Yo dieting does not work. It is too difficult to go for long periods of time without the foods you want and then to binge eat them when you slip up.

Instead, what I have found works best is not thinking about it as a "diet." **Rather, think about it as a lifestyle—the way in which you will live.** Because the word "diet" has so many bad feelings and emotions around it for most people, you will be more successful by not viewing your meal plan as a diet. The problem with diets is that they end. Remember the dietician I hired to create a "diet" for me for the 12 weeks leading up to my wedding? Well, he helped me lose 14 pounds. Guess what happened after I went off my diet. I gained 14 pounds in 14 days. I had restricted what I ate for what seemed like forever that I began eating too much once I was off the diet. I swung in the other direction because I was no longer on the diet.

Therefore, it is much easier to have some routines and rules in place which you follow 95% of the time. People often will say *"I dislike having rules because it is so constricting."* If you view it this way, then you are right. However, having some rules like the order you eat your food, ensuring you consume high-quality foods

95% of the time, how much you exercise, etc. actually free you up for other things. As mentioned in the routine chapter, once you have the routine and habit in place, it is so easy to maintain. The rules create freedom because you do not need to spend time and energy deciding on what you should and should not eat. **Rules make it easier to win.** These rules are better referred to as a "lifestyle." Something to do for the rest of your life.

You are one change away in how you view food and exercise from being able to be very fit. Do I still eat burgers, do I eat muffins, do I have cookies near Christmas? The answer is yes to every one of those questions. I have simply just taken the time to figure out my rules which allow me to enjoy life and allow me to feel good about my ability to perform on the soccer field and look good doing it.

After years and years of performing plastic surgery operations, Dr. Maxwell Maltz reveals in his best-selling book, *Psycho-Cybernetics*, that **a person always aligns with their self-image**. This is especially important. People who believe they are overweight can make the choices of an in-shape person over the next few weeks, but they always "snap back" to their view of themselves. Therefore, if they view themselves as a person who will always be overweight, then they make the same poor eating choices and lack of exercise that they always have.

Make sure that you take a minute and ask yourself what your views are related to food, how you feel, how you look, and if you weigh the right amount or too much. Now, it is not to say that it is only "in your head." Saying this would be a bit insulting. Instead, it is based on thought patterns that, when changed, will bring the results you want. As an example, I mentally view myself as someone who will always be healthy and fit. I changed my self-image before I got fit to help achieve the body that I wanted.

To make it easier to align with a "fit" self-image, a trick is to focus on the foods you like. Of all the vegetables out there, my three favorites are carrots, lettuce, and sautéed onions. I love fruits, meats, and most grains/carbs. So, what did I do to be successful? I set up my lifestyle and meal plan focusing on the things I enjoy. Will you ever see me eating an artichoke? Nope. Artichokes disgust me and make my taste buds hurt just thinking about it. Being able to find healthy foods you like will make it winnable to achieve a better self-image.

In conclusion, this chapter is all about challenging how you view your self-image and your lifestyle. If you view it as *"I should be on a diet,"* then you will probably fail. Instead, if you view your food choices as finding what you enjoy and creating a lifestyle, then you will be on your way to success. Having the self-image of a healthy and physically fit person is a great thing. Finally, eating healthy does not need to be difficult; on the contrary, when you eat healthier, all the foods you eat taste better. Imagine eating a slice of watermelon, or another fruit you enjoy. It tastes surprisingly good, right? Now, imagine eating a slice of watermelon after eating two candy bars. It will not taste so good because your taste buds have become used to the sugar rush from unhealthy sweets. Therefore, if you eat healthier foods, then when you eat fruit, it will taste like candy.

Chapter 4

Pre-Game and In-Game Nutrition

Your pre-game meal(s) can set you up for success or can cause you to fail. A person eating a meal comprising steak, cottage cheese, whole milk, cheese, and cashews will have different energy levels than the person who eats carrots, watermelon, fish, and rice before a game. Therefore, let us break down the foods to include in the hours leading up to a game to ensure you have a ton of energy when you need it most.

What to Eat the Morning of a Game

Upon awakening, your body has used up most of its excess blood sugar stores (glycogen) throughout the night, so consume foods that are higher in carbohydrates. Examples are fruits, vegetables, and healthy grains such as quinoa, brown rice, sweet potatoes, steel-cut oatmeal, and organic whole grain bread.

These carbohydrates are beneficial to replenish your body's blood-sugar stores and give you the energy to help you function appropriately until your next meal. There is a common misconception in the athletic world that you are supposed to "carb up" the night before a game. For example, many teams will have a pasta dinner the night before a game, thinking this will help them obtain enough carbs to be fully fueled for the game the next day. It is true that eating some carbohydrates is a good thing before a training session, but you do not need to eat three bowls of pasta the night before a game. **Eating too many carbs the night before a game will increase the chances that they will be stored in the body as fat.**

Also, a good recommendation for the morning of a game is to a consume some protein. However, avoid dairy products! Furthermore, there are better options than nuts, seeds, and beans prior to your game. Instead, eat some eggs or faster digesting sources of protein like chicken, turkey, or fish. Personally, scrambled eggs work best for me because I can prepare them with onions (a vegetable) and make several servings at once. This is great to have as a healthy grab-and-go choice in the morning when you are often hurried and rushed to get out the door.

What to Eat as your Last Meal Before Your Game Starts

It is beneficial for you to consume carbs closer to game time, but this depends on how well your body digests food and how empty or full you prefer to be when playing soccer. **Often, one to three hours before the start of the game is an ideal time to take in more carbohydrates in the form of faster-digesting vegetables, such as carrots; fruits such as apples, bananas, or watermelon, as well as carbs such as quinoa, sweet potatoes, or brown rice. Furthermore, consume turkey, fish, or grilled chicken to ensure you have some protein too and to keep you fuller for longer.** One last thing to consider is that if there is ever a time to add salt to your meal, prior to a game would be the best time to do it. Your muscles need salts which contain minerals like sodium, potassium, and magnesium to contract and work correctly. So, before those long games or games in very warm temperatures, consuming a bit of salt will help your muscles function properly and help you retain more water to ensure you remain hydrated.

Pre-Game Supplement

Many soccer players do not drink a pre-workout/pre-game supplement. However, this is often to the detriment of the player because it can increase their performance by 10-15% and is often used by other players on the field. Many players use lesser versions of pre-workout blends such as carbonated soda pop or energy drinks. The problem with these is all the filler ingredients, artificial flavors, and synthetic preservatives which are not good for your health. You will read more about which pre-workout supplement to take in the next chapter, but understand that it is recommended, and I take one too.

In-Game Nutrition

In 95% of practices/games, you do not need in-game nutrition. **Drinking a sports drink on an extremely hot day when you have a game that lasts more than an hour is acceptable but for most games, you already have enough nutrition in your body if you ate well before the game.** Your body is comprised of 70% water, so drink plenty of it!

As you can see, there are several things to ensure you have energy on game day. Also, this same knowledge can be used when you try out for a team too. If you have a tryout coming up, consider grabbing the *Understand Soccer* series book, *Soccer Tryouts*, to learn all the things that will help you make the team and have confidence from the start without being nervous. For pre-game nutrition, remember that quicker digesting foods like poultry and fish, vegetables, fruits, and grains/carbs are your best bets prior to game time to ensure everything in your system is helping you perform at your peak. Consider a pre-workout supplement to use only before games to give you a boost and do not worry about in-game nutrition other than water.

YouTube: If you would like to watch a video on what to eat before soccer, then consider watching the *Understand Soccer* YouTube video: *What to Eat Before a Soccer Game*.

Chapter 5

Supplements

Pre-Workout/Game

Ever feel like you do not have enough energy to perform well on the field? Well, pre-workout supplements can give you the physical boost and mental jump start that you need. The decision on whether to take a pre-workout supplement prior to a game will vary from person to person. Personally, I will take a high-quality pre-workout supplement to give me additional energy during important games. It is important to have enough energy to show off your skills and abilities. However, given that I am not a licensed physician, please consult your doctor before taking a pre-workout supplement.

Also, keep in mind that at least 80% of the pre-workout supplements on the market are not recommended. They are filled with artificial colors, flavors, sweeteners, and typically have a lot of filler ingredients, which make it seem like you are getting more for your money. However, you are only getting a bunch of chemicals, which will lead to long-term problems.

Instead, go for a pre-workout supplement with only a few high-powered ingredients—the most important being caffeine. **Caffeine is a central nervous system stimulant, which gives you energy and mental focus. Caffeine takes effect about 45 minutes after you consume it.** While caffeine is helpful for your performance on the field, the effects of caffeinated beverages (e.g., tea, coffee, pre-workout supplements, energy drinks, or carbonated soda pop) lasts for 4-6 hours, so avoid consuming caffeine in the 6 hours prior to bedtime to minimize its impact on your rest.

One of my recommended pre-workout supplements is Pure Pump. Pure Pump has the trusted ingredients you want in a pre-workout supplement without any of the fluff. This product is for both males and females. I am not sponsored by this company; I just really like this product because they do not add unnecessary ingredients. Personally, I consume the unflavored version, but I recommend the flavored version because the unflavored version tastes a bit metallic. One scoop works well for children, and two scoops is the recommended serving size for an adult.

When you take any kind of pre-workout supplement, make sure to drink at least eight ounces of water with it.

Post-Workout/Game

Ever wonder what would help you best recover after a training session, practice, or game in that 30-minute window when your body really wants nutrition to grow stronger? **Well, foods that are good to consume after a game are foods high in carbohydrates and fast-digesting protein.** An example of a food that is easy to obtain is organic milk. Though the evidence shows altering views on lactose, having some organic milk or a whey protein shake with non-GMO dextrose is beneficial after a game. You want to take in enough carbohydrates to spike up your blood sugar after a practice, game, or workout so that your body uses the protein that you will take in.

In terms of a supplement to use, **whey protein <u>isolate</u> is recommended because it is one of the most bio-available and quickest digesting proteins.** (Whey protein <u>concentrate</u> is less expensive, but it has a lot of fat and lactose that can lead to smelly flatulence. Whey protein <u>hydrolysate</u> is the best, but it is almost double the price of whey protein <u>isolate</u>. Whey protein <u>hydrolysate</u> does not provide even close to twice the benefits of whey protein isolate and should only be considered if cost does not matter to you.) If you drink milk, it has milk protein, which is 20% whey protein and 80% casein protein. It is essential that if you have more physical activities later in the day, take in enough carbohydrates like dextrose, bread, rice, potatoes, pasta, and oatmeal to replenish your glycogen. It is critical to minimize the amount of fat and fiber that you take in during the post-workout 30-minute window because fiber and fat are slower digesting. They slow the absorption of vitamins, minerals, and nutrients. Avoid very dense foods like spinach or peanut butter unless there is absolutely nothing else that you can consume. Something healthy is better than nothing.

The other recommended post-workout supplement is creatine monohydrate. More than 1000 studies have shown that creatine is a top supplement for exercise performance. Creatine is a combination of three essential amino acids: glycine, arginine, and methionine. Consuming creatine increases your stores of phosphocreatine, which is a form of stored energy in the cells that helps your body produce more high-energy ATP. ATP is referred to as the body's "energy currency." When you have more ATP, you perform better during soccer. Creatine also helps several processes that increase muscle mass and strength and boost recovery. If you worry about taking something as foreign sounding as creatine monohydrate, then understand that there are one to two grams of creatine in a pound of beef, and varying amounts in other red meats, dairy, poultry, and fish.

If you want to figure out which supplement you are interested in, check out labdoor.com! They go through most supplements and do the research on which ones are healthy and which ones are not, so you can have more time for soccer.

General Health

To maintain health and wellness, the last two things to consider are a multivitamin, and a fish-oil supplement. Think of a multivitamin as "insurance." By following the tips in this book and eating healthy food (e.g., fruits, vegetables, meat, grains, and dairy), you will obtain the vitamins and minerals you need. However, just in case there is a certain food that you are not eating with nutritional value that is not found in other foods, a multivitamin can help make up for what your meal plan lacks.

Lastly, a fish oil supplement is good too. Fish oil has been shown to:
1. Support heart health.
2. Treat mental disorders.
3. Aid in weight loss
4. Support eye health.
5. Reduce inflammation.
6. Support healthy skin.
7. Reduce liver fat.
8. Reduce depression.
9. Reduce attention deficit disorders.
10. Improve asthma.
11. Help bone health.

In summary, a pre-workout supplement increases your energy for important games and tryouts. Post-workout supplements like whey protein isolate and creatine increase strength and muscle building while shortening the time to recover. Finally, a multivitamin acts as a great way to not worry about missing any key nutrients in your meal plan while fish oil helps with so many things that it is an important part of overall health and wellness.

Chapter 6

Post-Game Nutrition

After your game is done, and you took a post-game supplement, your body is primed to use the nutrition that you consume to repair itself and build your muscles. Soccer players have practice and/or games several times per week, so it is ideal to take in nutrition that will help your muscles recover faster and ensure that you are not fatigued before the start of your next game.

Consume a meal like the one you ate hours before the game started. Include one meat, one fruit, one vegetable, and one carb/grain to help your body recover from the intense game. If you do not feel that you worked hard enough in the game to eat all this food, then consider eliminating the carb/grain. **If you eat well after your game, then you will perform better, quicker, and more efficiently next time.**

Before bed, you want a slower digesting meal, so consume foods high in fiber, high in fat, and high in protein. Some things to consider eating are nuts, seeds, meat, different nut butters (almond, cashew, and to a lesser extent, peanut butter). Also, vegetables are always great to eat. Personally, I eat five servings of vegetables a day because they help keep you full for longer. Vegetables contain vitamins, minerals, antioxidants, and phytonutrients which help you recover quicker, keep you feeling better, and help to maintain steady blood sugar levels so your energy levels do not spike and crash. Additionally, if you choose to eat dairy products and are not lactose intolerant, then before bed is one of the two best times to consume them.

Cheese, Greek yogurt, whole milk (preferably organic), and cottage cheese will do a terrific job of supplying muscle-repairing nutrients to your body for most of the night. **Dairy's milk protein is made up of 20% whey protein, and 80% casein protein. Casein protein takes up to seven hours to digest, which makes it a great pre-bedtime protein to help your body recover and gain strength.** Avoid food with a lot of carbohydrates (i.e., carbs) right before bedtime because the carbohydrates can spike your blood-sugar, which can make it harder to fall asleep and increase the chances that the food you just ate will be stored as fat, rather than used as fuel.

Example Meal Plan for a 3 p.m. Game

Breakfast (8 AM):
3 eggs (protein & fats)
½ sautéed onion (vegetable)
½ cup of oatmeal (carb)
1 orange (optional fruit/carb)

Lunch (noon):
8 ounces of grilled chicken breast (protein)
1 cup of carrots (vegetable)
1 apple (fruit/carb)
1-2 slices of organic bread (carb)

Snack (as needed):

1 banana (fruit/carb)
2 organic rice cakes (carb)

Pre-Workout (30 mins before game time):
1-2 scoops of pre-workout (additional energy)
1-2 cups of water (muscle recovery and hydration)

Game (3 PM)

Post-Workout (5 PM):
1 scoop of whey protein isolate (muscle recovery and growth)
1-2 cups of milk or water (muscle recovery and growth)
5 grams of creatine (muscle recovery and growth)

Dinner (6 PM):
8 ounces of turkey, beef, chicken, or fish (protein & fats)
1 cup of broccoli (vegetable)
1 cup of blueberries (fruit/carb)
1 sweet potato (carb)

30 Minutes Before Bed (10 PM):
½ cup of nuts (protein & fats)
4 ounces of organic cheese (protein & fats)
1-2 cups of leafy greens (vegetable)
1 cup of Greek yogurt or cottage cheese (protein & fats)

Example Meal Plan for a Daylong Tournament with 3 Games

Breakfast (5:30 AM):

3 eggs (protein)
½ sautéed onion (vegetable)
½ cup of oatmeal (carb)
1 orange (fruit/carb)

Pre-Game (30 mins before game time):
1 scoop of pre-workout (additional energy)

Game (7 AM)

Snack (8:45 AM):
1 banana (fruit – carb)
2 organic rice cakes (carb)

Pre-Game (30 mins before game time):
½ scoop of pre-workout (additional energy)
1 cup of water (muscle recovery and hydration)

Game (11 AM)

Lunch (1:00 PM):
8 ounces of grilled chicken breast (protein)
1 cup of carrots (vegetable)
1 apple (fruit/carb)
1-2 slices of organic bread (carb)

Pre-Game (30 mins before game time):
½ scoop of pre-workout (additional energy)
1 cup of water (muscle recovery and hydration)

Game (3 PM)

Post-Game Shake (5 PM):
1 scoop of whey protein isolate (muscle recovery and growth)
2 cups of milk or water (muscle recovery and growth)
5 grams of creatine (muscle recovery and growth)

Dinner (6 PM):
8 ounces of turkey, beef, chicken, or fish (protein & fats)
1 cup of broccoli (vegetable)
1 cup of blueberries (fruit/carb)
1-2 cups of whole wheat pasta (carb)

30 Minutes Before Bed (9:30 PM):
½ cup of nuts (protein & fats)
4 ounces of organic cheese (protein & fats)
1-2 cups of leafy greens (vegetable)
1 cup of Greek yogurt or cottage cheese (protein & fats)

*Note: This is a great meal plan for an adult. If you are a child or are reading this to help your child, then cut the portion sizes roughly in half. Make substitutions where necessary based on food preferences. Each section is labeled (i.e., protein, vegetable, fruit, carb) to make it easier for you to switch out something you or your child does not like. For example, use fruit interchangeably and vegetables too (i.e., eating watermelon instead of a banana is terrific and so is eating celery instead of broccoli.)

YouTube: If you would like to watch a video on what to eat after soccer, then consider watching the *Understand Soccer* YouTube video: *What to Eat After a Soccer Game*.

Chapter 7

Ronaldo's and Messi's Meal Plans

For an effective meal plan, it is often important to look at some of the best players to uncover what they are eating and to use it as a guideline for what you should eat. Specifically, if you saw your favorite star eating junk food before games, you might be more likely to believe that eating healthily does not matter too much. However, if you see the best players having a well-balanced meal plan, then it is more likely that you will follow their advice to improve your game. Let us look at what Cristiano Ronaldo and Lionel Messi consume to stay at the top of their game. For Cristiano Ronaldo, we will look at what he eats over the course of a typical day. For Lionel Messi, you will read how he changes up his meal plan depending how far away is his next big match.

Cristiano Ronaldo's Daily Meal Plan

From extensive research of Cristiano Ronaldo's eating habits, as shown in the images on his Instagram account, he divides his daily food intake into five to six smaller meals to prevent weakness or hunger throughout the day and provide protein to ensure he can maintain and build muscle. His favorite source of protein is seafood, but he also consumes protein shakes, steak, turkey, chicken, and eggs too. **Ronaldo changes his breakfast foods depending on the demands of training/games**, but he has been known to eat whole-grain cereal, egg whites, fruit juice, coffee, cold cuts, cheese, avocado toast, and fruit. For his first snack of the day, Ronaldo often enjoys fish and bread.

For lunch, Ronaldo likes fish or chicken, whole-wheat pasta or a baked potato, and green vegetables. For his second snack of the day, he keeps it quick by consuming a protein shake to promote muscle recovery after his vigorous training. For dinner, Ronaldo often enjoys his favorite meal of Bacalhau à Brás. It is a Portuguese dish made from salted cod, onions, potatoes, scrambled eggs, black olives, and fresh parsley. From time to time, Ronaldo also eats salads, rice, and beans. Again, he does not consume all these foods in one sitting, but he does eat high-quality foods like these to ensure that he performs well and recovers quickly.

Now, though this is a nutrition book, do not be misled into believing that he eats nothing unhealthy because he will celebrate birthdays with cake and occasionally has chocolate too. Therefore, if 95% of your meals are healthy, a slice of cake will not hold you back too much. However, should you want to avoid eating junk foods, you will have an advantage over those who do. **Also, because one of the main concepts of this book is to make things winnable, consider having dark chocolate instead of**

milk chocolate to make sure you are getting plenty of antioxidants while you satisfy that chocolate craving. Similarly, find organic cake mix when baking a cake to know that the ingredients are better than the generic pre-made cake which has 50+ ingredients—many of which are difficult to pronounce.

Lionel Messi's Weekly Eating Plan

Now, let us break down Lionel Messi's meal plan, according to Men's Health Magazine. **A week before a match, Messi decreases his carbohydrate intake and increases the amount of protein and water he consumes.** Also, Lionel Messi eats vegetable soup with spices at the beginning of meals. Some spices Messi uses are chili powder, coriander, ginger, and turmeric. Without as many carbohydrates, Messi may experience slightly less energy in the days leading up to a game. Cutting carbohydrates forces his body to become more efficient with the sugar levels in his blood.

Once Messi reintroduces carbohydrates a day before the game and on the day of the game, it increases his energy because of the carb loading. Messi's ideal dinner the day before a game contains meat (e.g., fish, chicken, or prawns), green veggies, an orange, and potatoes. Six hours before match time, Messi eats porridge and egg whites. Then, 90 minutes before the game starts, Messi eats fruit. Now, do you need to go to this extent by starting a week before each game to see results? Probably not. However, understand that the more you take eating seriously, the more it will help improve your in-game performance.

So, do you see any similarities between Ronaldo and Messi? They both eat healthy foods knowing that it will fuel their performances to ensure they will be the best. If you are wondering how top athletes like Cristiano Ronaldo train in the gym and on the pitch, be sure to grab the *Understand Soccer* series book, *Soccer Fitness*. Here is a summary of Ronaldo's & Messi's meal plans should you want to glance back at them quickly:

Cristiano Ronaldo

Sample Breakfast:
Whole-grain cereal, egg whites, and fruit

Sample Snack #1:
Tuna roll with lemon juice

Sample Lunch:
Chicken salad, green vegetables, and a baked potato

Sample Snack #2:
Protein shake

Sample Dinner:
Turkey, beans, rice, and fruit

Lionel Messi

<u>1 week before a big match</u>:
Meat (fish, chicken, or prawns)
Green veggies
Vegetable soup with chili powder, coriander, ginger, and turmeric

<u>The day before a big match</u>:
Meat (fish, chicken, or prawns)
Green veggies
Orange
Potatoes

<u>Six hours before match time</u>:
Porridge
Egg whites

<u>90 minutes before the game starts</u>:
Fruit

YouTube: If you would like to watch a video on what Lionel Messi eats leading up to a game, then consider watching the *Understand Soccer* YouTube video: *<u>Lionel Messi Meal Plan</u>*.

YouTube: If you would like to watch a video on what Cristiano Ronaldo eats throughout a day, then consider watching the *Understand Soccer* YouTube video: *<u>Cristiano Ronaldo Eating Diet</u>*.

Chapter 8

What to Eat on Non-Training/Playing Days

After reading about foods to eat before and after training, let us discuss what to eat on non-training days. A non-training day is an off day where you do not have weightlifting, practice, intense conditioning for at least 30 minutes, or a match. On these days, you need less energy from food but still want to avoid being hungry and recover fully.

Dairy (cheese, Greek yogurt, whole-fat milk, and cottage cheese) takes a long time for your body to digest, so the best times for a soccer player to eat it are as part of your last meal of the day after all activity or on off days where you are not training. Milk sugar, lactose, is a complex sugar which is tough to digest and more time consuming than simple sugar for your body to breakdown. Also, since milk protein is 80% casein protein, which is the slowest digesting protein that takes up to 7 hours to digest, it is best to avoid dairy before physical activities. Remember, food is fuel. Be sure to use the quicker digesting foods before and immediately after games and keep the slower digesting food for when you go long periods without eating, the most obvious one being when you go to sleep.

You will learn more about the macronutrients I aim to eat on off days, but I eat fewer carbs since I do not need as much energy on off days. Furthermore, I eat more fat to ensure I stay full, even though I have consumed less food. Similarly, I tend to eat around 3,600 calories per day on days I exercise and only 3,000 calories on days I do not work out to ensure my body has the energy to perform when I am competing. So, what does this mean for you? **Well, be sure to eat more food on training days to improve performance and help recovery but reduce the amount you eat on off days to ensure you stay at a good body composition.**

Additionally, the reason you want to eat more fats is not only to stay full, but to fight inflammation. Inflammation occurs in your joints, ligaments, tendons, spine, etc. anytime activity occurs. So, after days where you exercised intensely, your body will be suffering from inflammation which creates physical pain and increases the time your body should spend resting instead of preparing for the game you love. As a result, eating more inflammation fighting fat will make it easier to become fully recovered and get back on the field. According to *Harvard Health Publishing*, trans fats increase inflammation in the body, so we want to focus on the unsaturated fats with anti-inflammatory properties, according to the *American Journal of Clinical Nutrition*.

Consume fats like nuts, fish/fish oil, and olive oil to fight inflammation.

Nuts like almonds, walnuts, and pistachios are high in protein, fat, and fiber and have unsaturated fats, which help lower your bad cholesterol and raise your good cholesterol. **Fish oil has omega-3 fatty acids, which help keep your blood-fat levels in a good range, reduce stiffness, lessen the effects of asthma, increase focus, and decrease joint pain.** Lastly, a study published in the *Journal of Nutritional Biochemistry* found that the oleocanthal in olive oil had a significant impact not only on chronic inflammation but also on acute inflammatory processes, similar to the effects of nonsteroidal anti-inflammatory drugs (NSAIDs) like aspirin or ibuprofen (Motrin/Advil). Therefore, you can obtain the same inflammation-reducing properties from olive oil as the unnatural, over-the-counter medications, which have negative long-term side effects, especially on your liver.

Furthermore, if you are a person who is always looking for ways to get an edge over your competition, stretching on your off days is a great way to keep your muscles flexible, have healthy joints, reduce your chance of injury, and improve recovery. **Stretching helps in the recovery of muscles by lengthening them and increasing the amount of blood flow to them to take**

away the lactic acid. Lactic acid is created when you use your muscles past the point they are used to working, which creates muscle soreness the next day or two. If learning more about stretching interests you to improve your recovery and dominate on the pitch, then grab the *Understand Soccer* series book, *Soccer Fitness,* to learn more. Also, very mild exercise like walking will help to rid your body of its soreness too.

In summary, the best time to consume dairy is as part of your last meal of the day assuming you are done with all physical activity or are on an off day. Off days are a great time to reduce your carbohydrate intake because you need less energy. Furthermore, eating more fat on off days in the form of nuts, fish/fish oil, and olive oil will help you remain full and decrease the amount of inflammation in your body which lengthens the time it takes for you to fully recover and get back on the field. Lastly, a bit of stretching and walking will go a long way to helping to improve blood flow to your sore muscles which will cut your recovery time significantly.

Chapter 9

Sports Drinks vs. Water?

So how much water should you drink? According to the National Collegiate Athletic Association (NCAA), here is the recommended amount of water to consume for a college athlete. Reduce the portion size depending on your age:

When:	Ounces:	Ounces-to-Bottles:
2-3 Hours Before Activity	16 ounces	About 1 Regular-Sized Bottle
15 Minutes Before Activity	8 ounces	About 1/2 Regular-Sized Bottle
During Activity	4 ounces every 15-20 minutes	About 2-3 Large Gulps (1/4 of a Regular-Sized Bottle)
After Activity	16-20 ounces	1 to 1-1/4 Regular-Sized Bottles or 1 Large Bottle

Remember, how much you should consume depends on the weather conditions, and your level of activity on the field. Specifically, if you are a goalkeeper playing in the cool weather of a late-fall game, then drinking a lot of water is not as important. The colder temperature will limit the amount you sweat, and goalkeepers are the least-active players on the field. However, if you are an outside midfielder who runs a ton, and you are playing in the hot summer sun, then you should double or triple the amount of water you consume at halftime during a game.

When you sweat and do physical exercise, your body uses electrolytes. Although that may seem like a complex word, an electrolyte is a type of salt. Sodium, potassium, chloride, calcium, magnesium, and phosphate are all common components of electrolytes. **Electrolytes are essential for nerve and muscle function; they participate in regulating bodily fluids, and they help control blood pressure.** With this knowledge, many companies have created products aimed at aiding athletic performance. In theory, these drinks should help improve your performance, but let us look at what is really in a sports drink, and whether drinking one while playing helps. Here is the label of a bottle of the leading sports drink brand:

Nutrition Facts

1 servings per container

Serving size	Bottle (1g)

Amount Per Serving

Calories 140

	% Daily Value*
Total Fat 0g	0%
Saturated Fat 0g	0%
Trans Fat 0g	
Cholesterol 0mg	0%
Sodium 270mg	12%
Total Carbohydrate 36g	13%
Dietary Fiber 0g	0%
Total Sugars 34g	
Includes 34g Added Sugars	68%
Protein 0g	0%
Vitamin D 0mcg	0%
Calcium 0mg	0%
Iron 0mg	0%
Potassium 80mg	2%

*The % Daily Value (DV) tells you how much a nutrient in a serving of food contributes to a daily diet. 2,000 calories a day is used for general nutrition advice.

Ingredients: Water, sugar, dextrose, citric acid, natural and artificial flavor, salt, sodium citrate, monopotassium phosphate, modified food starch, glycerol ester of rosin, blue 1.

The Good:

It has water and a few electrolytes (salt, sodium citrate, and monopotassium phosphate).

The Bad:

Sugar – It has a lot of sugar which is only helpful if you are exercising strenuously for at least 60 minutes or more.

Dextrose – A faster-digesting form of sugar that is immediately usable by your body. Again, unless you are exercising intensely for at least an hour, you do not need it.
Citric Acid – Adds flavor and acts as a preservative.
Artificial Flavors – Synthetic chemicals that cost less to produce than finding natural sources.
Modified Food Starch – Most commonly derived from genetically modified corn, then altered to give it a more desirable texture.
Glycerol Ester of Rosin – a synthetic oil-soluble food additive known as "E445" used to keep oil in suspension in drinks.
Blue 1 – Linked to damaging chromosomes which is your genetic material. Each colored sports drink has a different dye which negatively impacts your health.

Next, the *British Medical Journal* has published many articles revealing the truth about sports drinks. Specifically, drink when you are thirsty and do not waste your money or calories on sports drinks—water is the better choice instead. The *British Medical Journal* team uncovered that sports drink makers spent a lot of money sponsoring less-than-rigorous research which suggested thirst was not a good guide to hydration and casting doubt on water as the beverage for staying hydrated. According to Fortune Business Insights, they expect the sports drink market to reach $32.61 billion by 2026. **Therefore, the same companies that are telling us water is not good enough are the same companies that profit when we purchase their sports drinks.**

In summary, water is the doctor recommended drink of choice for athletes. Avoid the overpriced sugar water with a few different types of salts which do not benefit you much and have a lot of unhealthy filler ingredients. Drink as you are thirsty to ensure you remain hydrated.

Chapter 10

General Nutrition Tips

This chapter is a catch-all for things that should be in this book but do not need an entire chapter themselves.

1. Eat your food in order.
2. Food on-the-go.
3. Stay away from alcohol, smoking, drugs, processed food, and fast foods.
4. Use the best salt.
5. Glass containers > plastic containers.

First, most people are only concerned with eating healthy foods, but they do not think about the order in which they should eat the healthy food. Say you have a healthy meal of organic bread, broccoli, chicken, and a banana. Most people eat the bread first because they have not eaten in a while, and their blood sugar is low. They eat most of the bread prior to starting on the other parts of their meal. They take bites of everything; sadly, the broccoli is the last food finished because they know it is healthy, but it their least favorite thing on their plate. **Eating in the order of carb, fruit, meat, vegetable is terrific either right before a game or immediately after a game to increase your energy levels for soccer or increase your blood-sugar levels after a workout to ensure that you use more of your meal to rebuild your muscles.**

However, eating in this order is not optimal for the meals that are far from physical exercise. If you are hours away from exercise or a soccer practice/game, then you should reverse the order in which you eat your food. **You should eat in order of vegetable, meat, fruit, grain. This ensures that you will**

consume the slower-digesting foods first. This will reduce the chance of a blood-sugar spike and ensure that you have a steady stream of energy for the next several hours, prior to eating your next meal. If you eat in the opposite order, and you consume the faster-digesting grains/carbs and fruit first, then your blood sugar will spike, more of the food may be stored as fat, your blood sugar will dip dramatically, and you will become exhausted and have limited energy for the next few hours, until you eat again.

Explained more scientifically, the higher the blood-sugar (i.e., glucose) level in your body, the more insulin your pancreas releases to balance your blood-sugar levels. Insulin also breaks down fats and proteins for energy. **If your pancreas releases a lot of insulin, then it will begin breaking down all your food very quickly, thus giving you a lot of energy for an hour or so. This is great if you will play soccer but bad if you will not be active, because you will feel a large energy crash.** Rapidly changing blood-sugar levels can cause serious long-term health problems, like diabetes.

Second, make eating healthy winnable. By having food to grab on-the-go, you increase the chances you make the right food choices. If you are a parent reading this book, consider grabbing the *Understand Soccer* series book, *Soccer Parenting*, for immediately usable information to help your soccer player perform better on the field and to boost your confidence helping them with soccer, even if you have never played before yourself. Here is a chart of healthy foods ready to eat or that take minimal preparation; You will notice that most of the snacks are fruits and vegetables:

Protein Bar	Banana	Blackberries	Pineapple	Parsnips
Organic rice cakes	Apple	Blueberries	Apricot	Cauliflower
Non-GMO Popcorn	Orange	Strawberries	Pear	Mushrooms
Almonds	Grapes	Raspberries	Tomatoes	Broccoli
Peanuts	Raisins	Cherries	Peppers	Carrots
Cashews	Peach	Cranberries	Cucumber	Radishes

Third, there are several things that will make it harder to be a success in soccer and life. **The activities that will prevent you from being the best player you can be are drinking, using drugs recreationally, and smoking.** These are must-avoid habits as they will force you to spend time, money, and mental energy on things other than soccer and impact your health and endurance on the field. Also, though not as obviously bad for you, processed foods and most fast-food restaurants will only slow you down. Fries and a burger before a game or boxes of processed food will only limit your energy, slow your growth, reduce your performances, and reduce your body's ability to recover. If you must eat processed foods, aim to eat the organic options. If you must grab fast-food, then stick with Chipotle or Panera Bread.

Fourth, most people think there is little difference between types of salt. For the soccer player who needs salt to stay hydrated and ensure their muscles can function properly, knowing your salts is helpful. Sea salt and table salt have similar composition, as they are both mostly sodium chloride. **Standard white table salt from salt mines is about 98% sodium chloride with the remaining 2% being anti-caking agents, chemical additives, sugar (dextrose), with no trace minerals.** They often use harsh chemicals and extreme heat when stripping away the trace minerals. Excitingly, sea salt comes from evaporated sea water. As a result, the two types of salt differ in their components, taste, and texture. According to Western Analysis, Inc., sea salt has up to 75 minerals and trace elements, making it healthier to eat than table salt.

Himalayan pink salt contains up to 84 different trace minerals. Depending on which source you read, Himalayan pink salt contains up to 15% trace minerals. **Lastly, remember that salt is still salt, just like a box of organic cookies is still a box of cookies.** Therefore, use salt sparingly. The typical American diet includes a lot of it already. Usually, I never add salt to my cooking—except for occasionally adding Himalayan pink salt to my scrambled eggs and sautéed onions on the morning of an intense workout or soccer game.

Fifth, glass containers are a better way to store and transport food. **Most foods come in plastics that contain hormone-disrupting compounds, like bisphenol-A (BPA), which have qualities that mimic the female hormone, estrogen.** Researchers at Exeter University in London studied the blood and urine of 94 teenagers aged 17-19 and found 80% had hormone-disrupting chemicals in their bodies. Bisphenol-A (BPA) can lead to conditions like cancer, thyroid disorders, and obesity. These compounds can travel into your food especially when you heat plastic containers, so never place plastic in the oven or microwave—even if the container claims to be oven/microwave safe. Therefore, stick with glass containers if you prepare meals in advance. I prefer glass containers with snap-on lids, as these keep the food fresher for longer.

Here is a quick recap of the various topics covered in this chapter for you to reference back to easily:

1. Food eating order - carb, fruit, meat, vegetable before and after activity. Vegetable, meat, fruit, carb when less active.
2. Make healthy eating easy by having healthy snacks on-hand.
3. Stay away from alcohol, smoking, drugs, processed food, and fast foods.
4. Himalayan pink salt > sea salt > table salt.
5. Avoid plastic containers.

Chapter 11

Weight Loss

Have you ever struggled with losing weight? Have you ever felt like if you dropped a few pounds, your confidence would increase? Well, this chapter is all about providing you tips and things to avoid if you are a soccer player who is interested in losing weight. Weight loss is a tough issue for most people, so this chapter reveals several things to consider so that you lose weight, and it does not return. Even if you are not interested in losing weight (and not all players need to), this chapter still has a ton of interesting information. Here are the things to watch out for when trying to lose weight:

1. Know how many calories to eat in a day.
2. Find your ideal body fat percentage.
3. Get a Fitbit.
4. Drink more water.
5. Get enough sleep.
6. Do not cut out all fat.
7. Do not go low carb on soccer days.
8. Avoid thinking there is a magic pill.

First, when starting a weight loss plan, it is important you understand what will happen when you get off the plan. Short-term weight loss will be maintained if you keep doing the things that allowed you to lose weight. **Whereas permanent weight loss requires a change in lifestyle to ensure you set up habits you can continue to do so you do not gain the weight back again.** Therefore, if there are certain weight loss things you really dislike doing, find more manageable activities which you can see yourself doing for the rest of your life. Also, competitive athletes need to lose weight differently than the average person. The average person can lose weight by fasting or cutting carbs, where as a soccer player would need to have a plan for weight loss to ensure they can perform on the field, by eating their allotted carbs around physical activity.

Weight Loss = Baseline Calories Needed + Exercise > Calories Consumed

Baseline calories are the number of calories your body would burn if you just laid in bed all day and did not move. To determine the number of calories you burned in a day, add the baseline calories to the amount of activity you did (i.e., walking, running, weightlifting, playing soccer, etc.) To lose weight, this number needs to be less than the number of calories you ate that day. **More simply, you lose weight by burning more calories than you eat.** To make it easy on yourself, go to the following website to let their calculator tell you how many calories you need to maintain your current weight and a breakdown of the macronutrients required for a person at your bodyweight.

https://www.active.com/fitness/calculators/calories

For example, at the time of writing this chapter, I am 6'0" tall and 195 lbs. I have an active lifestyle. The website indicates that it takes 3,400 calories to maintain my bodyweight. Also, it provides me a range of 383-553 grams/day of carbs, 85-298 grams/day of protein, and 76-133 grams/day of fat. Because I am always looking to add more muscle, I aim to eat at least one gram of protein for every pound I want to weigh. Therefore, I generally eat about 200 grams of protein per day. Next, I let the amount of activity I have that day determine the number of carbs I consume. On days where I am writing and working on publishing books or YouTube videos, I am less active and will consume less carbs because I do not need as much energy and I also eat more fat, so I stay full. Therefore, on inactive days, I will eat about 350g of carbs and 130g of fat.

My Inactive Days
200g protein x 4 calories/g = 800 calories from protein
300g carbs x 4 calories/g = 1,200 calories from carbs
120g fat x 9 calories/g = 1,080 calories from fat
Total = 3,080 calories (I eat less on days I am not active)

My Active Days
200g protein x 4 calories/g = 800 calories from protein.
475g carbs x 4 calories/g = 1,900 calories from carbs
100g fat x 9 calories/g = 900 calories from fat
Total = 3,600 calories (I eat more on days I am highly active)

Because 3,500 calories are roughly the number of calories in a pound, if I wanted to lose weight, I would need to eat less than the 3,400 calories needed to maintain my weight. Generally, trying to lose a pound a week (or be at a 500-calorie deficit each day) will make it manageable to achieve your goal weight without having to drop your calories and energy levels drastically. Remember that if you go back to your old habits, the weight will come back. **Almost always avoid focusing only on breaking a bad habit. Instead, replace the bad habit with a good habit.** For example, you get a sugar craving and have a bad habit of eating chocolate. A better habit would be to eat dark chocolate. A good habit when a sugar craving strikes is to eat a piece of fruit.

Second, as a soccer player with muscle, do not worry so much about your Body Mass Index (BMI) because body fat is a better way to measure your health. Doctors, dieticians, and nutritionists often judge whether a person is overweight by their BMI, but this is a scale better used for people who do not exercise. BMI treats fat and muscle the same which is not too helpful for a soccer player who has muscle mass which the average person does not. Therefore, unless you become inactive, avoid using BMI as a measure of success. A better guide is how your body looks in the mirror and what is your body fat percentage.

Using myself as an example, I have a BMI of 27, which would place me in the "overweight" category. However, I play soccer about two times per week right now and weightlift 3-4 times per week. I have visible abdominals, and a low body-fat percentage. Therefore, using myself as an example, it is easy to see that the BMI scale is faulty for someone who exercises regularly and weight trains often. Still unconvinced? Well, Cristiano Ronaldo is 6'2" and at peak condition he is 188lbs, but he is considered overweight too, which we both know is laughable!

Therefore, use the Body-Fat Rating Chart below, which applies to adults ages 18 and older, based on findings from the American College of Sports Medicine, the American Council on Exercise, and various other scientific studies. It will better help determine if you have a fit physique:

Body Fat Rating	Women	Men	Fitness Level
Risky - Low	<15%	<5%	Unsafe - See a Licensed Health Care Professional
Ultra Lean	15-18%	5-8%	Elite Athlete
Lean	19-22%	9-12%	Optimal Health and Longevity
Moderately Lean	23-30%	13-20%	Good Health
Excess Fat	31-40%	21-30%	Excessive Fat
Risk - High	>40%	>30%	Unsafe - See a Licensed Health Care Professional

Use the same website mentioned previously to determine your body fat by entering your weight, waist circumference, hips circumference, wrist circumference, and forearm circumference. Sure, there are more precise ways to measure than this method, but this will give you a great estimate of your current body fat percentage:

https://www.active.com/fitness/calculators/calories

Third, purchase a Fitbit/step counter/activity tracker. The recommended minimum of steps per day is 8,000, but a 10,000-12,000-step minimum is better if you are trying to lose weight. Walking burns the same number of calories as running, it just takes a little longer. **Getting enough steps is one of the most underrated things for weight loss.** Think about it, soccer players get a lot of steps, which helps explain why they are often one of the leanest athletes on the planet. If you are interested in more exercise tips to make sure your body is fit for game time and to give you a ton of self-confidence, then grab the *Understand Soccer* series book, *Soccer Fitness*.

Fourth, drink more water to flush out toxins from your body and improve digestion. Beverages like juice, carbonated soda pop, and alcohol have "stealth calories." These calories come in mostly undetected by our bodies. **Scientific evidence confirms that although high-calorie beverages count towards our daily calories, the body does not detect them the same way as it would recognize solid food.** By consuming solid food, people's bodies naturally compensate by reducing the remainder of their food intake. However, when people ingest liquid calories, they do not compensate for them by eating fewer calories. Richard Mattes, M.P.H, R.D., a professor of foods and nutrition at Purdue University says, *"Fluid calories do not hold strong satiety properties, do not suppress hunger and do not elicit compensatory dietary responses. When drinking fluid calories, people often end up eating more calories overall."* This explains the results of a study by researchers from Harvard University and the Children's Hospital in Boston that found women who increased their intake of sugar-sweetened beverages, gained significantly more weight than those who did not.

Fifth, obtain enough quality sleep. Too little sleep means more hours of the day awake. More waking hours generally results in more opportunities to eat food because your body is more likely to be hungry from increased waking hours. More food means more calories, which makes it difficult to lose weight. **Furthermore, not enough sleep over the long-term increases the hormone, cortisol, in your body which enlarges your appetite and increases your stress levels.** If you ever feel you have a hard time falling asleep or have a tough time staying asleep, invest in the *Understand Soccer* series book, *Soccer Sleep*.

Sixth, do not cut all fat from your meal plan. **You need fat to use the fat-soluble vitamins A, D, E, & K properly. Also, fat helps with satiation—the feeling of fullness.** In an interview with *Men's Health Magazine*, nutritionist Jaime Mass, R.D. said, *"When you remove fat from a food product, it must be replaced with other ingredients to provide a tasty and profitable alternative. So, if you take a food with fat, remove it, triple the carbs, double the sugar, add extra ingredients to support the consistency and flavor, label it fat-free and consume it for years and years, you are setting yourself up to be overweight and develop health problems, including abdominal fat, Type 2 diabetes, and cardiovascular issues."*

Even worse, processed foods like low-fat ice cream and low-fat yogurt typically contain more sugar and calories than their full-fat counterparts. Being fat-free is perfectly fine for foods like vegetables and most fruits because these are naturally fat-free. There is no processing that needs to occur to remove fat. However, avoid picking fat-free versions of food which naturally have fat in them. Personally, when I first started changing the way I ate, I cut nearly all fat from my meal plan because it made sense that fat makes you fat. However, this left me somewhat frail and very pale. Luckily, as I read and learned more, I realized the need for the macronutrient fat in a meal plan to ensure fullness and health for the person looking to lose weight.

Seventh, avoid low-carb diets like the ketogenic diet. Low carb diets are more reasonable for people who are not athletes, as they have less need for energy providing carbohydrates. As a soccer player, being in ketosis, a state where you are using fat as your primary fuel for energy, will not result in good performances on the field or training sessions. You need carbs to fuel your training and games. **If anything, reduce your carb intake on days where you do not play or have practice, but limiting carbs will make your body more lethargic on the soccer field.** The only carbs you should be interested in cutting are white bread, white rice, white potatoes, white pasta, and white sugar. These and other refined grains are low in nutrients whereas whole-grain bread, oatmeal, sweet potatoes, and brown rice are high in fiber and rich in B vitamins. Avoid an unbalanced meal plan and instead select one where you have a balance across all three macronutrients of protein, carbohydrates, and fat.

Eighth, avoid thinking there is a "magic pill" which you can take that will do the work for you. Thinking there are magic pills is not good because you develop the habit of looking for the easy way out. Thinking there are "overnight successes" is just as problematic because you do not see the 10 or so years of hard work that person did to become successful. **Leave the mindset of finding a magic pill and becoming an overnight success to other people who wish everything were easier.** The trick is knowing that things rarely get easier, you simply get better.

In conclusion, remember the following pointers to ensure you do not fall into weight loss traps which so many other people do:

1. Determine how many calories you need in a day.

2. Aim for an ideal body fat percentage.
3. Invest in an activity tracker to count your steps.
4. Avoid drinks with calories.
5. Get enough sleep.
6. Avoid fat-free foods or a fat-free diet.
7. Eat plenty of carbs on days you train or play soccer.
8. Avoid looking for magic pills and overnight success.

Chapter 12

How to Read a Nutrition Label

Nutrition Facts

4 servings per container

Serving size	1 Taco (1g)

Amount Per Serving

Calories 460

	% Daily Value*
Total Fat 25g	32%
Saturated Fat 15g	75%
Trans Fat 1g	
Polyunsaturated Fat 5g	
Monounsaturated Fat 4g	
Cholesterol 200mg	67%
Sodium 800mg	35%
Total Carbohydrate 32g	12%
Dietary Fiber 1g	4%
Total Sugars 5g	
Includes 4g Added Sugars	8%
Sugar Alcohol 1g	
Protein 27g	54%
Vitamin D 0mcg	0%
Calcium 0mg	0%
Iron 5.4mg	30%
Potassium 470mg	10%
Vitamin C	35%

*The % Daily Value (DV) tells you how much a nutrient in a serving of food contributes to a daily diet. 2,000 calories a day is used for general nutrition advice.

When reading nutrition labels, the trick is to buy items that do not require nutrition labels, like bananas, avocados, apples, celery, etc. This way, you can be confident that you are getting only what you want, and not all the fillers and unhealthy ingredients which help them last months or even years on a store shelf.

However, there will be times when you will need to buy something with a nutrition label on the back. Therefore, this chapter reveals how to look at a nutrition label as an athlete. As an example, I will use a nutrition label from a popular fast-food taco chain.

Firstly, the top of the nutrition label reveals the serving size and servings per container. **Often, when you are looking at the** nutrition label of an unhealthy food, the manufacturer will make the serving size tiny, so all the numbers on the label do not look so bad.** For example, the manufacturer of a small bag of chips will say that one serving is 1/3 of the bag. But who only eats 1/3 of a small bag of chips?

Now, let us talk about calories, and calories from fat. Sadly, many people still believe that eating fat will make you fat. Fat contains nine calories per gram—unlike protein and carbohydrates, which have four calories per gram. Therefore, fat can add up quicker, but it is still vital for many fat-soluble vitamins, testosterone production, energy, and to protect your organs. **If you track your calories, this section will help you, but remember that eating higher-quality and healthier foods will go a long way towards leading a healthy lifestyle.**

Below the %Daily Value* shows the percentage of the daily values of fat, cholesterol, sodium, carbohydrates (carbs), and protein from the food. Notice the "*" asterisk at the end of %Daily Value*. **If you look farther down on the nutrition label, it explains that the "*" asterisk is showing that the above percentages are the recommendations for a person who consumes 2,000 calories per day.** Remember the charts from health.gov back in chapter one which showed the guidelines for how many calories to consume based on your age and level of activity? For a young soccer player who trains and plays several times per work, 2,000 calories are reasonable. However, for an active 16-year-old, 2,000 calories would not be enough. Not eating enough calories would leave them without enough energy in games and may result in weight loss, depending on their current size. Therefore, keep in mind how many calories you should eat to determine if the %Daily Value* applies to you or if you need to make some slight adjustments to make the numbers more relatable.

Continuing in this same section, the label lists fats, carbs, and proteins because they are the three food-related macronutrients. It also lists cholesterol and sodium because food manufacturers are required to point out these, since a large portion of Americans struggle with consuming too much sodium and have high cholesterol levels. **Sodium (e.g., table salt) makes food taste better and acts as a great preservative, so food manufacturers put large quantities of salt in their products to improve their taste and shelf life.** Some sodium (and potassium, calcium, magnesium, etc.) is necessary for the proper functioning of a hard-training soccer player's muscles. However, because there is so much salt in processed foods (e.g., pretzels, ready-to-eat meals, frozen dinners, take-out, etc.), you should not add salt to them.

An April 2017 study published in the *Journal of Clinical Investigation* confirmed that increased salt intake leads to water retention and increased appetite. Interestingly, your body tries to maintain a sodium/water ratio similar to sea water. When you consume sodium, your body holds on to water to maintain the right ratio. Consuming a single gram of table salt causes your body to retain up to an extra four cups of water, which equals roughly one pound.

Drinking more water flushes out the extra sodium, returning water levels to normal, and helps you lose water weight. You can use this knowledge to your benefit by avoiding extra salt to ensure you do not become bloated because of water weight. Also, you can consume more salt and water prior to going out in extremely hot temperature weather to ensure you have more water in your body to remain hydrated during those summer games. This will give you an advantage over your competition as they become dehydrated from the intense heat. Sadly, a high-sodium diet causes more than just water weight gain; it also increases blood pressure and increases your risk of a heart attack or stroke. Heart attack is the leading cause of death for both women and men in the United States, while strokes are the third-leading cause of death.

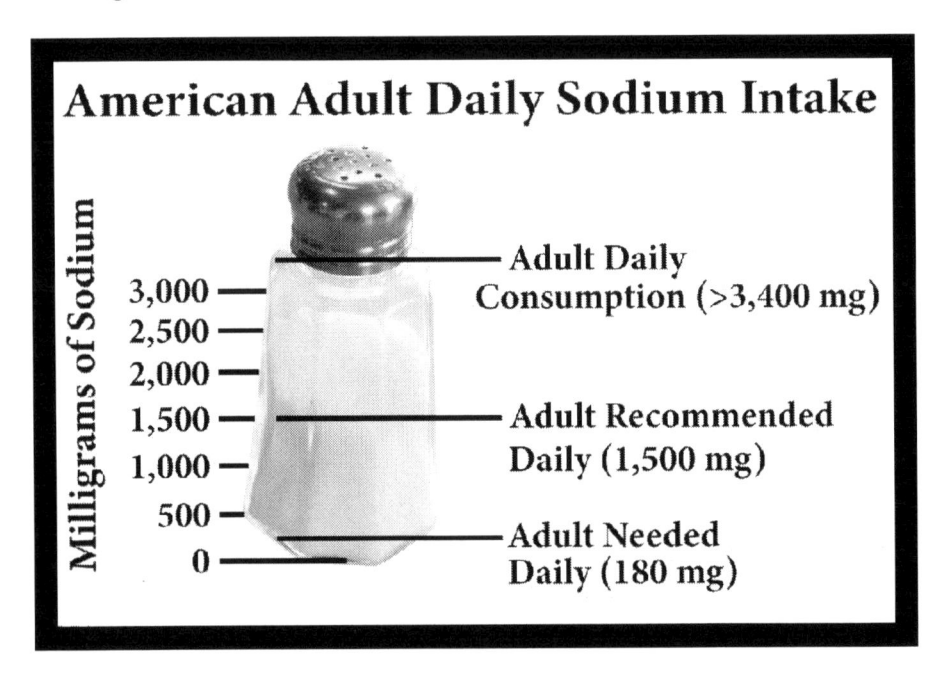

American Adult Daily Sodium Intake

Milligrams of Sodium

- 3,000 — Adult Daily Consumption (>3,400 mg)
- 2,500
- 2,000
- 1,500 — Adult Recommended Daily (1,500 mg)
- 1,000
- 500
- 0 — Adult Needed Daily (180 mg)

You can also notice what to expect when scanning through the ingredients at the bottom of the nutrition label. Trans-fat is a definite no-no. Many countries have banned trans-fat. There are some naturally occurring trans-fats in cheese, milk, and meats that are not too worrisome. **However, you should avoid hydrogenated oils because they increase your bad cholesterol (LDL) and decrease your good cholesterol (HDL).** If there is less than .5g of trans-fat in food, then the food manufacturer can round it down to 0g. Again, this is another reason that food manufacturers often suggest smaller serving sizes.

Also, the new guidelines set forth by the Food & Drug Administration (FDA) require food manufacturers to reveal the amount of sugar that they add to their product. Furthermore, when looking on the label under carbohydrates and you notice there is sugar alcohol, it is an easy tell that there has been processing of the food. The more processing the worse. **Sugar alcohols are popular, low-calorie sweeteners which are partially resistant to digestion. Sugar alcohol causes bloating, diarrhea, and smelly flatulence.**

The FDA recommends much less protein than a hard-training soccer player needs for muscle repair and growth. The general guideline for a hard-training athlete is based on how much you want to weigh. If you want to weigh 150 pounds, then I recommend you consume 150 grams of protein per day.

The label also lists some major micronutrients, and the number of grams of fat, cholesterol, sodium, and carbs which are recommended to eat if you consume 2,000 or 2,500 calories per day. **Once you know your numbers, you can quickly look past the micronutrient and calorie section when viewing nutrition labels.**

Finally, let us look at the ingredients of these tacos. The things to look for when reading an ingredient list are:
1. What is the number of ingredients?
2. Are there words you cannot pronounce?
3. Are there artificial or genetically modified ingredients?

> **Ingredients:** Seasoned Beef: Beef, water, seasoning [cellulose, onion powder, salt, maltodextrin, soy lecithin, tomato powder, sugar, spices, citric acid, caramel color, disodium inosinate & guanylate, natural and artificial flavors, modified corn starch, lactic acid, yeast], salt, phosphates, iceberg lettuce, enriched white flour, shortening (partially hydrogenated soybean oil and hydrogenated cottonseed oil), salt, chili powder, onion, natural flavor, xylitol, sugar, baking soda, sodium acid pyrophosphate, dough conditioner (mono- and diglycerides, enzymes, wheat starch, calcium carbonate, potassium sorbate), Cheddar cheese (cultured pasteurized milk, salt, enzymes, annatto), Cheese Sauce: Nonfat milk, cheese whey, canola oil, food starch, contains 1% or less of vinegar, lactic acid, potassium citrate, potassium phosphate, sodium stearoyl lactylate, citric acid, cellulose gum, yellow 6.

First, for tacos, you should see ingredients like beef, turkey, chicken, or pork, lettuce, tomato, onion, cheese (milk, salt, enzymes), avocado, whole grain wheat, etc. These are all ingredients that you can pronounce. However, when you look at the taco ingredients on the label provided, you will see a lot more. **The large number of ingredients is a huge sign that plenty of them are bad.**

Second, the harder the ingredient is to pronounce, the higher the chance that it is not good for you. On the ingredient list, we see things like disodium inosinate, disodium guanylate, artificial flavors, partially hydrogenated soybean oil, hydrogenated cottonseed oil, xylitol, sodium acid pyrophosphate, mono- and diglycerides, potassium sorbate, potassium citrate, and sodium stearoyl lactylate. These are all hard to pronounce for most people and yep, you guessed it, they are not good for your health either.

Third, are there artificial or genetically modified ingredients in the food? Much of the health/fitness community has differing opinions on genetically modified food. There is another chapter explaining them, so I will reveal why they are not good later in this book. **However, more of the hard-to-pronounce ingredients are**

also artificial. Also, there are easier-to-pronounce ingredients, like soy lecithin, maltodextrin, modified corn starch, sugar, canola oil, and vinegar which are often created from genetically modified foods like soy, canola, corn, and sugar that are sprayed with weed killers that are harmful to your health.

Additionally, when you see colors (e.g., Yellow #6) listed as ingredients, you know the product is likely not good. The U.K. and many countries have already banned food colors, but the U.S.A. is well behind the times. Researchers at Southampton University found that consuming certain synthetic dyes increased hyperactivity in kids. Also, a different U.S. study done in *Science* magazine found that children who consumed a food-dye blend performed worse on a test, as compared to another group who drank a placebo drink right before the test instead. Blue #1, Blue #2, Red #2, Red #3, Green #3, Yellow #5, Yellow #6, and Red #40 are examples of the dyes to stay away from. These can cause many types of cancer, attention disorders, chromosome damage, tumors, violent behaviors, asthma, poor sleep, allergies, and eczema.

In conclusion, knowing what to look for on a nutrition label and ingredient list will make it easier to select healthier options. Also, knowing exactly which problems, disorders, and diseases are caused by artificial and poor-quality ingredients will makes you less likely to want to eat junk food. **A pro-tip is to stay along the perimeter aisles of a grocery store and avoid going up and down the inner aisles.** The perimeter contains most of the fruits, vegetables, meats, and dairy—many of which have no nutrition labels. The inner aisles contain the highly processed foods, which all have nutrition labels because the food manufacturer must legally tell you what is in their product. Like a doctor uses X-rays to see what is going on in your body, you can use nutrition labels and ingredient lists to see what is in your food.

Chapter 13

Organic, GMO, Vegan/Vegetarian, Gluten-Free, and Paleo Diets

Has one of your friends ever started a new diet, and you wondered what they could eat? Well, this chapter discusses many mainstream diets and provides insights on the potential benefits of eating organic food.

When it comes to nutrition, you have heard a hundred times that "you are what you eat." Something you may have never heard is that **you are what your food eats,** too. Therefore, it is vital that you have high-quality food. If the cow, chicken, pig, turkey, or fish that you are eating consumed nutritious food, too, then those animals will provide more nutritional value than poorly fed animals. **This food will be much more vitamin-rich, nutrient-dense, and mineral-packed.**

Not all vegetables are created equal. Although plants do not eat other food, they do absorb nutrients from soil, and if you consume genetically modified food, then it will lack most of the rich nutrients found in organically raised fruits, vegetables, and grains. The most genetically modified foods on the market are sugar, canola, cottonseed, soy, squash, zucchini, alfalfa, and corn. These are foods for which scientists often modify to withstand harmful weed killers, which can be cancer-causing to humans. Although fewer weeds are good in theory, using harmful and synthetic weed killers to achieve it is not good. **Weed killers function as mineral chelators, which make it so that the plant sprayed with weed killer does not take as many of the nutrients from the soil.** Therefore, the same amount of protein, fat, and carbohydrates are in a genetically modified ear of corn; however, genetically modified corn has a lot less nutritional value, which is especially important for an athlete.

Organic foods are much more expensive, but they are a healthier option. If organic food is not in the budget, do not worry as there are thousands of professional soccer players who do not eat organic foods, yet can still succeed on the field. Your ability to pass, dribble, shoot, and defend are much more important for improving as a soccer player than consuming organic food over conventional options.

Organic meat, poultry, eggs, and dairy products come from animals that were not given antibiotics or growth hormones. Organic plants are grown without using most conventional pesticides, synthetic fertilizers, bioengineering, or ionizing radiation. **Organic foods do not have hidden ingredients and are not made by synthetic farming techniques. In most organic foods, what you see is what you get.**

If you are interested in some organic foods but are not willing to change everything you put in your fridge, the best places to start are:

1. Dairy
2. Fruits or vegetables that do not have a peel
3. Most frequently genetically modified foods

First, organic dairy like whole milk not only tastes richer, but it does not have added growth hormones and is less likely to upset a person's stomach given that many people have a hard time processing milk sugar, lactose.

Second, based on an analysis of test data from the U.S. Department of Agriculture, here is the full list of the dirty dozen fruits and vegetables which are great to consider eating organic:

1. Strawberries
2. Spinach
3. Kale
4. Nectarines
5. Apples
6. Grapes
7. Peaches
8. Cherries
9. Pears
10. Tomatoes
11. Celery
12. Potatoes

Third, sugar, canola, cottonseed, soy, squash, zucchini, alfalfa, and corn are the most often genetically modified foods on the market. Therefore, consider organic options instead to ensure you are consuming food which will improve your performance and not hold you back.

Next, becoming a vegetarian has become popular in recent years in the United States of America, though it dates back as early as 700 B.C. Let us discuss the different kinds of vegetarians, and the health concerns related to some types of vegetarians. **Keep in mind that this information is meant for soccer players who want to improve their nutrition for better performance and more self-confidence.**

Some of the different types of vegetarians are:

1. Vegetarian – Avoid meat, poultry, game, fish, shellfish, or by-products of animals.
2. Lacto/ovo vegetarian – Avoid all animal flesh but do consume dairy (lacto) and egg (ovo) products.
3. Vegan – Vegetarians who avoid all animal and animal-derived products as food or for other uses. This is the strictest type of vegetarian diet.

4. Pescatarian – Do not technically meet the common definition of vegetarian, but they follow a semi-vegetarian diet by eating fish and other seafood but no poultry or meat.

Why does 8% of the world's population follow a vegetarian diet? The three main reasons are for spiritual beliefs, health-concerns, and not wanting to hurt animals. **Research shows that vegetarian and vegan diets are low in saturated fat and cholesterol. Additionally, vegetarian diets contain high amounts of vitamins, minerals, fiber, and healthy plant compounds from nutrient-dense foods, like fruits, vegetables, whole grains, nuts, and seeds.** However, the vegetarian diet can be problematic for a soccer player due to its low intake of some nutrients—particularly protein, iron, calcium, zinc, vitamin D, vitamin B12, and long-chain omega-3 fatty acids.

Lacto/ovo vegetarians and pescatarians rarely have the low intakes of the previously recommended key nutrients because they are obtained easily by consuming dairy products, eggs, and fish. **Therefore, vegans must meet their protein, cholesterol, and other nutrient needs by being very planned and making sure to eat a wide variety of peas, beans, lentils, chickpeas, seeds, nuts, organic soy products, and whole grains like wheat, oats, and brown rice.** Otherwise, low testosterone, hair loss, and bruising easily are likely to occur.

So, is it helpful for a soccer player to be a vegetarian? Well, you can get by if you are a pescatarian, lacto vegetarian, ovo vegetarian, or any combination of the three. If you are a vegan, then you must plan all your meals to ensure that you can obtain the nutrients which are not readily available from plants. Also, because these types of diets often have so little protein, it is less likely that you will build muscle as quickly as your competition, and your recovery will take longer. **Therefore, you will likely be better** off not being a vegetarian if improving your soccer game is your top priority.**

Like the vegetarian diet, the gluten-free diet has become very mainstream. Gluten is a substance that is present in grains, and it is responsible for the elastic texture of dough. Gluten is a general name for the proteins found in wheat, rye, oats, spelt, and barley. Not every grain contains gluten (e.g., rice and corn are gluten-free). Naturally gluten-free food groups include vegetables, fruits, meat, poultry, fish and other seafood, dairy, and nuts. **The proteins in wheat include gluten and wheat germ agglutin, which are lectins that make up the plant's natural defense system to fend off insects and humans.** These lectins are inflammatory and immuno-disruptive, which result in a negative reaction, ranging from very mild (e.g., no signs of discomfort or pain) to very severe gastrointestinal problems due to gluten intolerance (e.g., people with celiac disease that are allergic to gluten).

For the soccer player, many processed food products on grocery-store shelves contain gluten, so by not eating processed foods, you are well on your way to becoming healthier by avoiding many of the unhealthiest foods in the store. **However, unless you are allergic to gluten, do not let the minor inflammation that can occur from wheat to deter you from organic whole wheat breads or oatmeal which provide plenty of other vitamins and a lot of quality carbohydrates to fuel your performances on the field and when you work out.**

The last mainstream diet we will discuss is the Paleo diet (also known as the "Paleolithic diet", "Stone Age diet", "hunter-gatherer diet", and "caveman diet"). **It is a meal plan based on the human diets of those who lived several thousand years ago, who consumed only foods that could be gathered or hunted.** A Paleo diet typically includes lean meats, fish, fruits, vegetables, nuts, and seeds. Therefore, foods that are farmed (e.g., dairy products, legumes, and grains) cannot be consumed on this diet. This diet can be effective for a soccer player if they consume a lot of fruit to obtain the carbohydrates needed to fuel their physical activity. However, not eating dairy or farmed grains (e.g., sweet potatoes, brown rice, oatmeal, whole-grain bread, and whole-wheat pasta) will leave you with a bit less energy than your competition, and it will take longer to recover after training.

In conclusion, this chapter's purpose is to reveal the different mainstream diets and how they impact a soccer player. In all honesty, other than eating organic foods, many of the diets discussed in this chapter are not likely the best for a soccer player because they make it difficult to obtain one of the key macronutrients. Therefore, if your number one goal is great on-the-field performances, then certain diets may hold you back. In the vegetarian diet, it is difficult to get enough protein. In the Paleo and gluten-free diets, it is more difficult to obtain the carbs needed to fuel your practices and games. In a previous chapter, we discussed the fat-free diet which does not provide enough fat to help with recovery, feeling full, and effectively using the four fat-soluble vitamins.

Chapter 14

Herbs and Spices

When preparing food, it is important to balance healthy with tasty. Sure, eating barbeque sauce may be tasty, but often is not healthy. Eating food plain is healthy, but unless you are buying expensive cuts of meats and perfectly preparing your food, the food will not be too tasty. That is where herbs and spices benefit you. They merge health benefits with improved taste. Also, if you struggle with some physical pains, then use many of the herbs and spices in this chapter to reduce it. Either by taking a vitamin blend that has many herbs and spices or by incorporating it into your cooking, you will ensure that you make adding herbs and spices a habit and an easy way to boost your health and recovery. If your parents or someone else does the grocery shopping, there is a ready-to-use product mentioned at the end of this chapter that they can purchase that will help significantly.

Spice: Turmeric

What it does: Turmeric treats a variety of conditions such as arthritis, joint pain, diabetes, digestive issues, and cancer.

What foods to add it to: It is great in grain dishes (brown rice, quinoa, couscous, etc.), sauces, curries, and smoothies.

Spice: Black Pepper

What it does: Stimulates the digestive enzymes, which enhances food absorption. If you eat enough nutrients but your body cannot absorb them, then you are wasting money and some of the benefit of the food. Therefore, your body can obtain the nutrients it needs by eating more of them or being better able to use the ones it is already receiving from the foods you eat regularly. Also, black pepper has been found to have anti-tumor properties because it protects against oxidative damage by free radicals.

What foods to add it to: Use this spice in soups, salads, meat, grain dishes, eggs, potatoes, and more. One of the great things about black pepper is you can generally find it anywhere you go. Some other herbs/spices are hard to find in a restaurant or at a friend's house, but black pepper is in most places.

Spice: Cinnamon

What it does: Cinnamon improves digestion, prevents diabetes, fights infection, manages blood sugar, increases focus, and benefits cholesterol levels. Spiking and dipping blood sugar levels can drive hunger and cravings. The antioxidant compounds in cinnamon help prevent those spikes and dips by improving the way your cells metabolize blood sugar.

What foods to add it to: Use cinnamon on oatmeal, porridge, when cooking bread, toast, applesauce, apples, sweet potatoes, smoothies, cereal, cottage cheese, coffee, or plain Greek yogurt.

Spice: Garlic

What it does: Though it is not technically an herb or spice, garlic and garlic powder are great to use when cooking. Garlic reduces high cholesterol and helps with blood pressure management. Garlic destroys cancer cells and disrupts the metabolism of tumor cells, says Karen Collins, R.D., nutrition advisor to the American Institute for Cancer Research. She says, *"Studies suggest that one or two cloves weekly provide cancer-protective benefits."*

What foods to add it to: Personally, I buy a 3-pound bag of pre-peeled garlic from Costco and place it in the freezer to make it last a long time. Next, I will add to chicken, tacos, vegetable sautés, guacamole, salsas, salads, etc. Also, I will take a clove every morning, chew it, and then wash it down with water as part of supplement portion of my "morning habit mastery." If you do not have a routine for how to get a terrific start to every day, I would suggest the *Understand Soccer* series book, *Soccer Mindset*, which reveals habits to do most mornings that will give you a competitive advantage over your competition.

Spice: Ginger

What it does: With its antioxidant and anti-inflammatory properties, ginger has been used to remedy nausea, bloating, gastrointestinal discomfort, morning sickness, chemotherapy-induced nausea, weight loss, and soreness from workouts. A study found that when consuming one teaspoon of ground ginger daily for 11 days, participants experienced a 25 percent reduction in exercise-related muscle pain compared with those taking a placebo. The gingerol in ginger blocks nerve pathways which process pain.

What foods to add it to: Add ground ginger to healthy pancake, waffle, or muffin batter. Sprinkle the spice over applesauce or toast with peanut butter. You can even buy ginger root, cut off a little piece, and take it as part of your supplement routine.

Spice: Oregano

What it does: Oregano contains vitamins A, C, E, and K, as well as fiber, folate, vitamin B6, iron, calcium, magnesium, and potassium. This herb is rich in antioxidants and has anti-microbial, anti-inflammatory, and anti-cancer properties.

What foods to add to: Sprinkle oregano on fish, chicken, roasts, stews, soups, vegetables.

Spice: Cayenne Pepper

What it does: Capsaicin, the compound that gives cayenne its burn will increase your body's metabolism and help you burn more fat. Purdue University researchers found that people who added half a teaspoon of this spice to a meal ate 70 fewer calories at their next meal and craved less fatty and salty foods.

What foods to add it to: Popcorn, chicken, beef, curry, stew, chili, and Mexican food.

Spice: Paprika

What it does: Paprika is another capsaicin-containing spice derived from peppers. This ingredient has plenty of antioxidants that increase the spiciness of your food. Paprika acts as an antibacterial and stimulant which helps normalize blood pressure, improves circulation, and increases the production of saliva and stomach acids which aids digestion. Paprika also has a ton of vitamin A and contains some iron. However, avoid cooking it on high heat because it burns easily which changes its flavor and burnt foods/spices/herbs are carcinogenic (cancer-causing).

What foods to add it to: Grilled meats, eggs, soup, rice, and vegetables.

Spice: Nutmeg

What it does: Your mouth has a lot of bacteria, and nutmeg fights the germs with antibacterial compounds, which reduce plaque formation and cavity-producing microbes. Additionally, nutmeg is rich in protective anti-inflammatory compounds which can lower your risk of cancer.

What foods to add to: Add to chili, ground turkey, chicken, potatoes, carrots, pumpkin, winter squash, cabbage, broccoli, cauliflower, spinach, apples, bananas, peaches, nectarines, pears, pineapple, mango, scrambled eggs, omelets, pancakes, and French toast.

Spice: Cumin

What it does: The spice that makes Mexican food taste like Mexican food, cumin helps with weight-loss, prevents diabetes, and reduces the chances of getting cancer. Its medicinal properties come from its phenols and flavanols.

What foods to add it to: Add it to soups, stews, lentils, beans, rice, sausages, eggplant, lamb, pork, potatoes, and rice.

Spice: Rosemary

What it does: Rosemary contains vitamin A, vitamin B6, vitamin C, and other B vitamins such as folate and thiamin. It is high in fiber, has anti-inflammatory properties, and helps with digestion. Adding a bit to the meal plan is helpful for a little extra brainpower, focus, and mental clarity too.

What foods to add it to: You can brew rosemary in a tea to treat an upset stomach or nausea. Use rosemary with soups, stews, salads, chicken, lamb, pork, steaks, fish, grains, mushrooms, onions, peas, potatoes, and spinach. Rosemary oil is fantastic for skin, hair, sore spots, dryness, dandruff, and healing of cuts and bruises.

Herbs and spices add a ton of flavor, and a lot of health benefits to whatever you are cooking. Some people (me included) shy away from adding herbs and spices to food because they are afraid that they will mess up the dish. The trick is to not be afraid to experiment in your own home when no one else is eating the food. Instead of putting the herb or spice on all the food you prepared, just take one fork or spoonful of the food and add the spice to it. If it tastes good, then add it to the rest of the food, too. If it tastes bad, then try again with another fork or spoonful of the food you prepared, and a different herb or spice.

A few times experimenting in the kitchen will leave you healthier; you will recover from training easier, and you will enjoy healthier food options. **If buying all these different herbs and** spices seems overwhelming, then buy blended options, like salt-free Mrs. Dash, which has over 14 flavor varieties.

Chapter 15

Which Oils Should You Use?

With so many oils to choose from, it is difficult to know which one is best to use and if any of them will help you or hurt you as a soccer player. Some oils can help you shine, and others will leave inflammation in your body. Regardless, with all oils, a little goes a long way. Therefore, in this chapter we will discuss several oils and reveal the three you should use. These are listed roughly in order from most to least healthy.

Olive Oil

Choose an olive oil that is not overly processed. Extra-virgin olive oil has a better taste and more nutrition, as compared to refined olive oil. Extra-virgin olive oil contains unsaturated fats, which, according to multiple studies, promotes heart health. Olive oil has a low smoking/burning point, compared to other oils, so avoid cooking with it because by heating it, olive oil burns and makes it carcinogenic (cancer-causing). It is better to drizzle it on salads, pour it on rice, or use as a dip for bread.

Coconut Oil

Coconut oil is a bit of a controversial topic for many members of the health community. Due to its high saturated fat content, for a long time, people believed it was bad for your heart. Newer studies reveal that saturated animal fat differs from saturated plant fat. Coconut oil contains medium-chain triglycerides (MCTs) that are quick absorbing fatty acids that can increase the number of calories you burn. Also, these fats convert to energy easier, which makes them the ideal fat to eat before games. Also, coconut oil boosts your metabolism, curbs your appetite, and aids weight loss. One of my favorite treats is a piece of toasted bread. Let it cool for a few minutes, then spread a layer of coconut oil on the bread, followed by a layer of natural peanut butter. They combine very well and taste oddly like cinnamon rolls but without the unhealthy ingredients.

Here are some benefits of coconut oil:

1. Protects Your Skin from UV Rays
2. Increases Your Metabolism
3. Improves Your Dental Health
4. Relieves Skin Irritation and Eczema
5. Improves Brain Function
6. Moisturizes Your Skin
7. Helps Fight Infections
8. Increases Your Good HDL Cholesterol
9. Helps Reduce Belly Fat
10. Protects Your Hair from Damage
11. Decreases Hunger and Food Intake
12. Improves Wound Healing
13. Boosts Bone Health
14. Combats Candida
15. Reduces Inflammation
16. Natural Deodorant

17. Source of Quick Energy
18. Relieves Symptoms of Arthritis
19. Improves Liver Health
20. Soothes Chapped Lips

Avocado Oil

It is unrefined like extra virgin olive oil but has a much higher smoking/burning point and little flavor, making it great to cook with and use in stir-fry. Avocado oil is high in unsaturated fats and promotes healthy cholesterol levels and enhances absorption of nutrients, according to a review published in the May 2013 *Critical Reviews in Food Science and Nutrition*. Avocado oil contains vitamin E, but it is a little pricey. This heart-healthy oil has anti-inflammatory properties which help prevent arterial damage, heart disease, and blood pressure.

Ghee

Though not actually an oil, ghee is a form of clarified butter that has recently gained popularity with dairy-free eaters because the milk protein and lactose has been removed from the butter so people who are lactose-intolerant can usually eat it. It has fat-soluble vitamins with a more intense flavor than butter. Its high smoking point makes it good for cooking, but it normally is quite expensive. Therefore, grease your pan with it or use to butter bread.

Grapeseed Oil

Although often found in hair and skin products, grapeseed oil also has medicinal properties, which makes it useful as food, too. This is a great source of essential fatty acids and vitamin C. However, make sure to consume it in moderation because it also contains omega-6s, which can cause inflammation.

Sunflower Oil

This oil is high in vitamin E, has a high smoking point, and minimal flavor. Sadly, sunflower oil contains a lot of omega-6 fatty acids, which the body needs but are considered inflammatory, while omega-3s are anti-inflammatory. Sadly, many sunflower oil and sunflower seed producers use Neonicotinoids. This is an insecticide that kills our pollinating friends, the bees. Now, bees can sting you, which hurts, but getting rid of the world's best pollinator means you will not have the following foods at your grocery store, all of which need bees to grow:

Alfalfa, Almonds, Apples, Asparagus, Beans, Beets, Blackberries, Blueberries, Brussels sprouts, Buckwheat, Cabbage, Cantaloupe, Cauliflower, Celery, Cherries, Chestnuts, Chives, Clover, Cranberries, Cucumber, Currants, Eggplant, Flax, Garlic, Gooseberries, Grapes, Horseradish, Kale, Lettuce, Mustard, Onions, Parsley, Peaches, Pears, Plums, Pumpkins, Radishes, Raspberries, Rhubarb, Squash, Strawberries, Sunflowers, Sweet potatoes, Turnips, and Watermelon.

Peanut Oil

A staple of Asian cuisine, peanut oil has plenty of unsaturated fats to complement its nutty taste, nice smell, and proper use in cooking at hot temperatures. Peanut oil is high in omega-6s and impacts your omega 3:6 ratio, causing health problems. Only purchase the cold-pressed versions because the commercial peanut oils you find in grocery stores and fast-food restaurants are refined, bleached, and deodorized. Now, technically, peanuts are not a nut; they are a legume. Legumes are high in protein and fiber, but they contain some "anti-nutrients," such as phytic acid, that impair your absorption of nutrients. Therefore, eat legumes (e.g., peanut butter, peanuts, peanut oil, lentils, peas, and beans) in moderation.

Canola Oil

It is usually highly processed and derived from the genetically modified crop, rapeseed. It is used in many restaurants and fast-food chains. You are better off avoiding it.

Vegetable Oil

Vegetable oil is often a blend of canola, corn, soybean, safflower, and palm oils. You might see the word "vegetable" and think it must be good for you. Well, it is not. All vegetable oils are highly processed and have an imbalance in the recommended ratio between omega-3s and omega-6s. Vegetable oils are linked to cancer, and many other health-related issues. Also, the ingredients come from insect-repellant sprayed crops, and genetically modified organisms. To support this using the Sydney Diet-Heart study, two groups of adults consumed the same amount of oil and fat, but the first group's fat came from vegetable oil and margarine while the second group's fat came from sources like olive oil and butter. Everything else about their eating and lifestyles remained the same.

Both groups were evaluated regularly for the next seven years. The group that consumed more vegetable oil had a 62% higher rate of passing away compared to the group eating less vegetable oil.

Other Things to Watch Out for

Oils labeled as "partially hydrogenated" or "fully hydrogenated" are made from vegetable oils like soybean or cottonseed, according to the Center for Science in the Public Interest. These oils are trans fats which the Food & Drug Administration (FDA) says increase your risk for heart disease. Recently, the FDA ruled that manufacturers must remove all trans fats from their products.

In conclusion, there are many oils to use, but **the three to use as a soccer player are extra virgin olive oil, coconut oil, and avocado oil**. Use olive oil to dip bread, drizzle it on salads, or pour it on rice. Use coconut oil as an energy boosting oil before games. Use avocado oil to cook. Whatever oil(s) you end up choosing, store them away from direct sunlight to prevent oxidation. Here is a summary list of the oils in their general order of most healthy to least healthy:

Good:
1. Olive oil
2. Coconut oil
3. Avocado oil

Okay:
4. Ghee
5. Grapeseed oil
6. Sunflower oil
7. Peanut oil

Bad:
8. Canola oil
9. Vegetable oil
10. Hydrogenated oil

The following chart reveals the smoking point of different cooking oils. My recommendation is to not cook with any oils with a smoking point less than 450° to ensure that the oil does not burn and become harmful for your health. The smoking points in the image were determined by taking the average smoking points from these five sources:
1. What's Cooking America
2. Wikipedia
3. Centra Foods
4. The Spruce
5. Baseline of Health Foundation

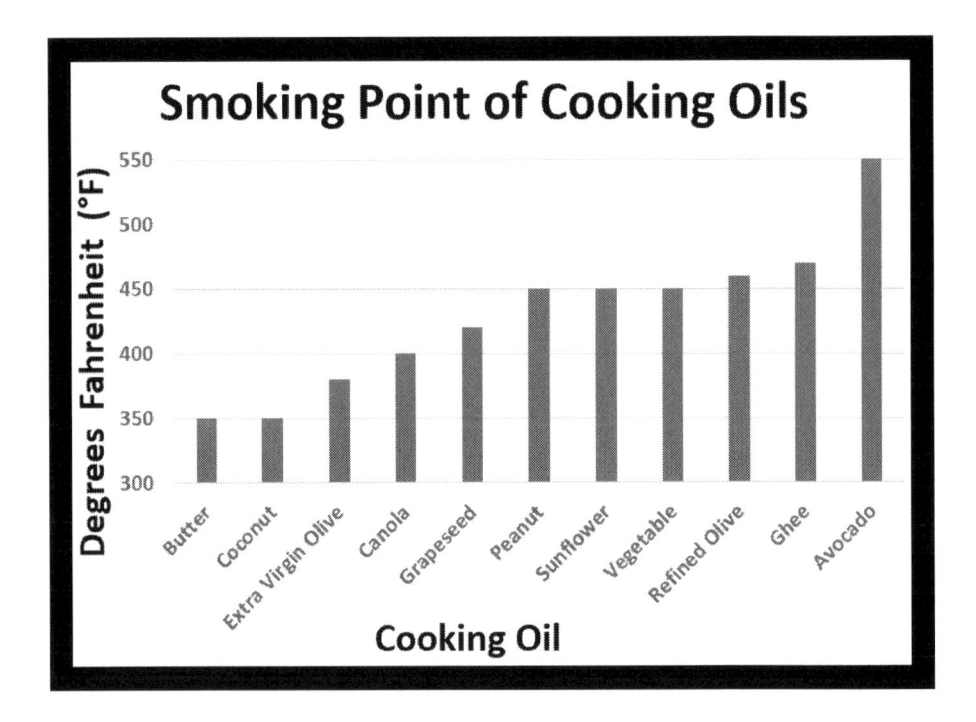

Smoking Point of Cooking Oils

Cooking Oil	Smoking Point (°F)
Butter	350
Coconut	350
Extra Virgin Olive	380
Canola	400
Grapeseed	420
Peanut	450
Sunflower	450
Vegetable	450
Refined Olive	460
Ghee	470
Avocado	550

Afterword

Congrats! Because you read this book, you gained a ton of knowledge on how to take your nutrition to the next level. Implement the tips mentioned to increase your energy, improve your recovery, and make a bigger impact on your team. Understand that my first meal plan looked much different than what I currently eat today, but I started somewhere and now is the time for you to start too.

Even more importantly, you have increased your confidence. This is huge! Just by reading this book and applying the knowledge within, you have given yourself a massive advantage over your competition. You have shown that you care about eating well for your soccer career and hopefully for the rest of your life. Great job!

Excitingly, that is what a book can do. A book takes a person's decades of experiences, highs, lows, and knowledge and then condenses that information down into something which you can read in a few hours. Think about it; you just spent a few hours learning what took me a decade to figure out. Because of that, I know you will use the knowledge to improve your nutrition dramatically.

If the tips you read in this book helped your nutritional knowledge, please leave a positive review letting me know on Amazon.com.

WAIT!

Wouldn't it be nice to have an easy one-page summary of the key points covered in this book? Well, here is your chance!

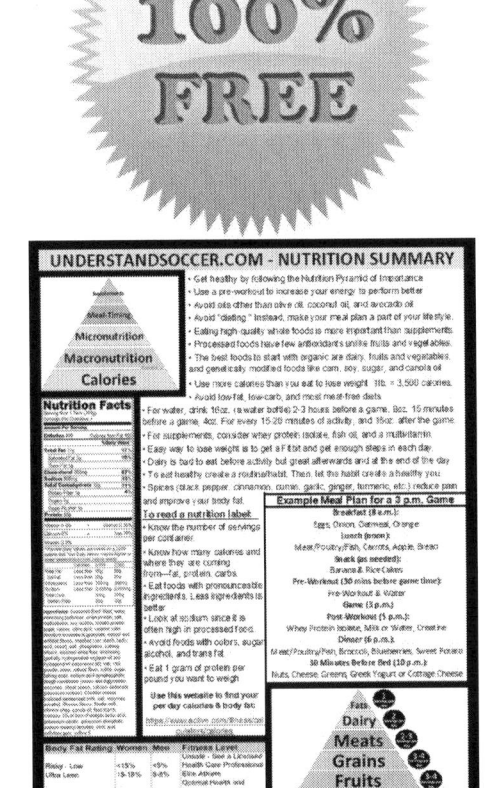

Go to this Link for an **Instant** One-Page Printout:
UnderstandSoccer.com/free-printout

This FREE checklist is simply a thank you for purchasing this book. This one-page summary will ensure that the tips in this book help you become the best soccer player you can be!

Free Book!

How would you like to get a book of your choosing in the *Understand Soccer* series for free?

Join the Soccer Squad Book Team today and receive your next book (and potentially future books) for FREE.

Signing up is easy and does not cost anything.

Check out this website for more information:

UnderstandSoccer.com/soccer-squad-book-team

About the Author

There he was—a soccer player who had difficulties scoring. He wanted to be the best on the field but lacked the confidence and knowledge to make his goal a reality. Every day, he dreamed about improving, but the average coaching he received, combined with his lack of knowledge, only left him feeling alone and unable to attain his goal. He was a quiet player, and his performance often went unnoticed.

This all changed after his junior year on the varsity soccer team of one of the largest high schools in the state. During the team and parent banquet at the end of the season, his coach decided to say something nice about each player. When it was his turn to receive praise, the only thing that could be said was that he had scored two goals that season—even though they were against a lousy team, so they did not really count. It was a very painful statement that after the 20+ game season, all that could be said of his efforts were two goals that did not count. One of his greatest fears came true; he was called out in front of his family and friends.

Since that moment, he was forever changed. He got serious. With a new soccer mentor, he focused on training to obtain the necessary skills, build his confidence, and become the goal-scorer that he had always dreamed of being. The next season, after just a few months, he found himself moved up to the starting position of center midfielder and scored his first goal of the 26-game season in only the third game.

He continued with additional training led by a proven goal-scorer to build his knowledge. Fast-forward to the present day, and, because of the work he put in, and his focus on the necessary skills, he figured out how to become a goal-scorer who averages about two goals and an assist per game—all because he increased his understanding of how to play soccer. With the help of a soccer mentor, he took his game from being a bench-warmer who got called out in front of everybody to becoming the most confident player on the field.

Currently, he is a soccer trainer in Michigan, working for Next Level Training. He advanced through their rigorous program as a soccer player and was hired as a trainer. This program has allowed him to guide world-class soccer players for over a decade. He trains soccer players in formats ranging from one-hour classes to weeklong camps, and he instructs classes of all sizes, from groups of 30 soccer players all the way down to working one-on-one with individuals who want to play for the United States National Team.

If you enjoyed this book, then please leave a review.

Additional Books by the Author Available on Amazon:

Soccer Dribbling & Foot Skills: A Step-by-Step Guide on How to Dribble Past the Other Team

Soccer Defending: A Step-by-Step Guide on How to Stop the Other Team

Soccer Coaching: A Step-by-Step Guide on How to Lead Your Players, Manage Parents, and Select the Best Formation

Soccer Mindset: A Step-by-Step Guide on How to Outsmart Your Opponents and Improve Your Mentality

Thank You for Reading!

Dear Reader,

I hope you enjoyed and learned from **Soccer Nutrition**. I enjoyed writing these steps and tips to ensure your food is giving you great performances and providing you energy.

As an author, I love feedback. Candidly, you are the reason that I wrote this book and plan to write more. Therefore, tell me what you liked, what you loved, and what can be improved. I'd love to hear from you. Visit UnderstandSoccer.com and scroll to the bottom of the homepage to leave me a message in the contact section or email me at:

Dylan@UnderstandSoccer.com

Finally, I need to ask a favor. **I'd love and truly appreciate a review.**

As you likely know, reviews are a key part of my process to see whether you, the reader, enjoyed my book. The reviews allow me to write more books. You have the power to help make or break my book. Please take the 2 minutes to leave a review on Amazon.com at: https://www.amazon.com/gp/product-review/1949511294/.

In gratitude,

Dylan Joseph

Glossary

Amino Acids – They combine to form proteins, the building blocks of life.

Antibiotics – Medicines that help stop infections caused by bacteria. They do this by killing the bacteria or by keeping them from copying themselves or reproducing.

Antioxidants – Slow or prevent damage to cells caused by free radicals, which are unstable molecules in your body.

Body Fat – A normal part of the human body that serves the important function of storing energy. Obesity is an excess of body fat frequently resulting in a significant impairment to health.

Body Mass Index – A weight-to-height ratio, calculated by dividing one's weight by the square of one's height and used as an indicator of obesity for non-athletes.

Caffeine – A compound that is found in tea and coffee plants that is a stimulant of the central nervous system and provides energy.

Calorie – A measure of how much energy food provides. It is the energy needed to raise the temperature of 1 gram of water through 1 °C.

Carbohydrates (Carbs) – A macronutrient broken down by the body to provide energy from sugars, starches, and cellulose.

Celiac Disease – An immune disorder in which people cannot eat gluten because it will damage their small intestine.

Cholesterol – A waxy, fat-like substance found in all cells of the body to make hormones, vitamin D, and substances that help you digest foods.

Cortisol – The "stress hormone" that can help control blood sugar levels, regulate metabolism, help reduce inflammation, and assist with memory formulation.

Creatine Monohydrate – Similar to endogenous creatine produced in the liver, kidneys, and pancreas that helps supply energy to muscle cells for contraction.

Dextrose – Also referred to as glucose and is a simple sugar.

DNA – The carrier of genetic information.

Electrolytes – Minerals dissolved in the body's fluids, creating electrically charged ions. The most important are sodium, potassium, calcium, magnesium, and phosphate.
Enzymes – Increase the rate of reactions with food in your body.
Fat/Lipids – A macronutrient to provide your body energy, support cell growth, protect your organs, keep your body warm, absorb fat-soluble nutrients, and produce important hormones.
Fat-Soluble Vitamins – Vitamins A, D, E, and K that dissolve in fats and oils. They can be stored in the body's fat stores.
Fiber – Important for regulating digestion, regular bowel movements, helps keep you feeling fuller for longer, improves your cholesterol levels, regulates blood sugar levels, and prevents diseases like diabetes and heart disease.
Fitness – Being physically fit and healthy.
Gastrointestinal – Related to the stomach and intestines.
Genetically Modified Organisms (GMO) – Organisms whose genetic material has been artificially manipulated in a laboratory through genetic engineering, which creates plants, animals, bacteria, and viruses that do not occur in nature or through traditional crossbreeding methods.
Gluten – A protein substance present in many grains and responsible for the elastic texture of dough. Gluten functions as a plant's natural defense system to fend off insects and humans from eating them.
Glycogen – Excess blood sugar stored in the body.
Growth Hormone – A hormone that stimulates growth in animal cells including muscles.
Himalayan Pink Salt – Salt containing up to 84 different trace minerals. It can be made of up to 15% trace minerals.
Hormones – A regulatory substance produced in humans and transported in tissue fluids such as blood or sap to stimulate specific cells or tissues into action.
Inflammation – The immune system's response to injury and infection to tell the immune system to heal and repair damaged

tissue, as well as defend itself against foreign invaders, such as viruses and bacteria.

Insoluble Fiber – Does not dissolve in water or in your body and remains unchanged as it moves through you before being pooped out. It acts as a cleaner that travels through your body scrubbing the walls.

Insulin – Regulates the amount of glucose in the blood.

Ketogenic – A low–carb diet emphasizing protein and fat and minimizing carbohydrates.

Lacto Vegetarian – Someone who does not eat meat or eggs, but who eats dairy products.

Lactose – Milk sugar made up of glucose and galactose.

Macronutrition – Fats, proteins, and carbohydrate required in large amounts in the diet.

Meal Timing – Planning meals and snacks for specific times throughout the day to manage hunger, improve performance, and help recovery.

Micronutrition – Vitamins and minerals needed in smaller amounts than macronutrients.

Minerals – Help with growth, bone health, fluid balance, and several other processes.

Nutrition – Food necessary for health and growth.

Nutrition Label – The nutrition information panel required on most packaged food in many countries showing what nutrients are in the food.

Organic – Generally, foods without the hidden ingredients and farming techniques that the government does not require manufacturers put on food labels. What you see is what you get in most instances.

Ovo Vegetarian – Someone who does not eat meat or dairy, but who eats eggs.

Paleo Diet – A meal plan based on human diets of those who lived several thousand years ago by consuming only foods that could be gathered or hunted like lean meats, fish, fruits, vegetables, nuts, and seeds.

Pescatarian – Someone who chooses to eat a vegetarian diet, but who also eats fish and other seafood. Often, they also eat dairy and eggs too.

Phytonutrients – Give fruit and vegetables their colors and help protect against diseases.

Preservative – Added to food to prevents the growth of microorganisms as well as slowing the oxidation of fats that cause food to expire.

Protein – A macronutrient made up of many amino acids that help aid in normal cell function, muscle growth, creating enzymes, producing hormones, and can be used for energy too.

Saturated Fat – Solid at room temperature and found in meats, coconut, and palm kernel oil.

Self-Image – The idea one has of one's abilities, appearance, and personality.

Smoking Point – The burning point/temperature at which an oil begins to degrade and become harmful for your health.

Sodium – A mineral found in salt that is abundant in nature and is used to flavor and preserve food.

Soluble Fiber – Dissolves in water and in gastrointestinal fluids when it enters your body's stomach and intestines. It changes into a gel-like substance that bacteria in your body digests.

Sugar Alcohol – Low-calorie sweeteners that are partially resistant to digestion and cause bloating, diarrhea, and smelly flatulence.

Supplement – A product taken by mouth that contains a dietary ingredient like vitamins, minerals, amino acids, herbs, and other substances.

Testosterone – A hormone that is the most potent of the naturally occurring androgens that cause strengthening of muscle tone and bone mass.

Toxins – Natural substances covering a large variety of molecules, generated by fungi, algae, plants, or bacteria metabolism. These have harmful effects on humans—even at very low doses.

Trace Minerals – You only need a small amount of these minerals, which include iron, manganese, copper, iodine, zinc, cobalt, fluoride, and selenium.

Trans Fat – Chemically created in a factory by hydrogenating oils and it is bad for your heart health.

Unsaturated Fat – Liquid at room temperature and considered beneficial fats because they can improve blood cholesterol levels, ease inflammation, stabilize heart rhythms, and play several other beneficial roles.

Vegan – A person who does not eat or use animal products including seafood, eggs, and dairy.

Vegetarian – Someone who avoids meat, poultry, game, fish, shellfish, or by–products of animals.

Vitamins – Necessary for energy production, immune function, blood clotting, and other functions.

Water-Soluble Vitamins – Vitamins B and C are not stored in the body, so they must be taken in daily.

Acknowledgments

I would like to thank you, the reader. I am grateful to provide you value and to help you on your journey of becoming a healthier and more energetic soccer player. I am happy to serve you and thank you for the opportunity to do so. Also, I would like to recognize people that have made a difference and have paved the way for me to share this book with you:

I want to thank the grammar editor, Abbey Decker. Her terrific understanding of the complexities of the English language ensured that the wording needed to convey the messages was appropriate and she provided countless grammatical improvements.

Also, I would like to thank the content editors Kevin Solorio, Toni Sinistaj, and Youssef Hodroj. They reviewed this book for areas that could be improved and additional insights to share that could immediately help you, the reader.

Many thanks,

Dylan Joseph

Made in the USA
Middletown, DE
23 November 2024